A Seal Called Andre

The Two Worlds of a Maine Harbor Seal

Harry Goodridge and Lew Dietz

Down East Books

Camden, Maine

Published by Down East Books
A wholly owned subsidiary of the Rowman and Littlefield Publishing Group, Inc.
4501 Forbes Boulevard, Suite 200, Lanham, Maryland 20706
www.rowman.com

16 Carlisle Street, London W1D 3BT, United Kingdom

Distributed by National Book Network

British Library Cataloguing in Publication Information Available

Library of Congress Cataloging-in-Publication Data Available

ISBN 978-1-60893-295-5 (pbk. : alk. paper)
ISBN 978-1-60893-269-6 (electronic)

♾™ The paper used in this publication meets the minimum requirements of American National Standard for Information Sciences Permanence of Paper for Printed Library Materials, ANSI/NISO Z39.48-1992.

Printed in the United States of America

For Thalice

Contents

Collaborator's Note

Although I am not truly a part of the story of Andre, I have been close to it from the beginning. Harry Goodridge and his family are my Rockport neighbors. I've known Harry and his wife, Thalice, more than thirty years, and their lively children from babyhood. And, of course, I knew Andre from the day he joined this unusual family as a bright-eyed little pup.

Thus, it seemed logical that I, a writer, should join with Harry in shaping the remarkable story of a Maine harbor seal who lives in two worlds and has come to think of himself as people. The experience was thoroughly pleasurable. Harry was easy to work with: He has the talent for almost total recall, and on the occasions when he missed something, Thalice in her quiet way filled in the gaps.

The children made contributions as well, dropping by at the house with fat morsels for the pot. Harry had his notes and a log that consisted of scribblings on fifteen years of calendars. Helpful, too, was a complete file of pertinent correspondence.

The deeper I got into the tale, the more I came to realize that while this was the story of Andre the seal, it was also very much the story of Harry Goodridge the man. Knowing Harry these many years helped me to understand something of the nature of this fellow who succeeded in maintaining a close relationship with a wild creature for fifteen years and in the process broke through the communication barrier that separates man from the fellow animals with which he shares the Earth. In his hunting days, I hunted with Harry and camped with him in the hills. He would head out alone in the morning, and I wouldn't see him again until dark. We got along fine, except that he never did learn to like my coffee.

So working together on a book was no more than a continuing association. My task was simply to sit in his office and draw out of him the facts and the juices and give them flavor. Our modus operandi was to meet before lunch. I'd warm Harry up with a few questions, and he would talk until I had all I could digest at one sitting. Harry was of the opinion he could do better before supper, over a few glasses of what he called "sneaky Pete." I was of the contrary opinion, and having a slim seniority, I prevailed. These sessions were taped for my reference. I would make a final draft of a chapter before we proceeded to the next.

This method of tying up as we went along was more or less forced upon us. The Goodridge children, all married except one, read the book in progress, and they came by every day or so, eager for the next installment. Although I couldn't possibly write fast enough to satisfy them, I found myself putting in longer hours than was my habit. I've heard it said that Dickens's fans lined up at the Battery in New York, waiting for the boat that would bring the next installment of *David Copperfield*. Our fan club of five was every bit as impatient for the unfolding of the Andre saga.

Although this is the story of one particular and rather special harbor seal, we did feel we should include what little is known about these neglected sea mammals as a species. Some marine mammalogists may not agree with some of Harry's observations and conclusions. This is fair enough. Harry doesn't agree with some statements made by members of the scientific establishment on the subject of seals. For example, there is the delicate matter of seal lovemaking. Some qualified marine mammalogists have stated that harbor seals copulate only at sea. A reasonable fellow, Harry will only say that if this is the truth, then Andre must be special, since he managed very well on a dock.

As for acknowledgments, we are indebted to scores of scientists whose papers on the Pinnipedia constitute the slim body of seal literature. In particular, we'd like to express our thanks to David Richardson, of the Department of Marine Resources, and to Gavin Maxwell, whose books we found both refreshing and informative. And, certainly, our thanks to Thalice, who stoutly aided and abetted our efforts.

And to the Goodridge children go special thanks. It was their enthusiasm that gave us the satisfaction of writing for an immediate and appreciative audience.

— Lew Dietz
Rockport, Maine, 1975

*(*Camden Herald*)*

1

The Arrival

There was something special about Andre from the beginning. He came to me out of the sea that day, fifteen years ago, as a dog comes to his friend and master, freely and without fear.

The place of our meeting was Robinson's Rock, a dark, weed-cloaked ledge in Maine's Penobscot Bay, four miles to seaward of my home in Rockport. I was with Bob Lane in his powerboat, for my own boat was laid up that morning, and Bob, a local boatbuilder, had offered to take me out.

We headed out in a flat calm. The bay is normally calm in the morning; the breeze will pick up in the afternoon as the sun warms the earth. It was one of those warm, hazy southwest days. I suppose only Maine people know what is meant by a "southwest day" or a "northwest day." A southwest day is soft, the horizon smoky; a northwest day is clear, bright, and cool.

I have lived all my life near the sea. I can't imagine myself living anywhere else. Inland people live in the midst of change they can do nothing about. The sea you can count on; it will always be there. Petty problems may be thorning you ashore, but once you head out into the bay, you are able to shuck everything off. The sea is a sanctuary.

Robinson's Rock is one of the many seal "haul-out" locations in the bay. These are places where harbor seals go ashore at low tide to sun and rest. I was looking for a seal pup that day. It would be my third. I had lost the first two—one because of my ignorance, the other from what in nature's terms must be called "natural causes."

I was resolved that this time nothing would go wrong. Armed with some hard-earned knowledge, I was optimistic about finally establishing a close and long-term relationship with one of these little-understood marine animals.

My earlier attempts to establish such a relationship had been prompted by curiosity and an itch for submarine companionship. Although I earn my basic income as an arborist—the fancy name for tree surgeon—I'm also a professional scuba diver. I'm called upon to locate lost moorings, untangle lines from propellers, and repair underwater gear. And I've spent many an unpleasant hour searching for the bodies of the drowned.

I also spend a lot of time at what might be called recreational diving. I enjoy exploring the strange and beautiful underwater realm, gathering scallops and—in the days when it was legal—lobsters. I've been called a loner, and maybe I am. I have no objection to people, but I must admit I relate better to animals. Perhaps it's simply that animals act sensibly. For years I'd been savoring the thought of exploring the undersea world with a creature whose natural element it is.

Over the years I'd observed these sleek, beautifully adapted sea mammals around the outer ledges, both at play and in a serious search for food. I'd admired them the way a Little Leaguer might admire a Major League ballplayer. In the sea, man is a clumsy amateur; the seal is a pro.

Frequently on my cruisings I would come face-to-face with

one of these engaging fellows. Suddenly a droll, bewhiskered face would pop up out of the sea, part of a head as smooth as a cannon-ball. He would appear wary but at the same time curious.

"Who are you, funny creature?" the child-wise eyes seemed to inquire.

Despite the shabby treatment the seal has experienced at the hands of man, he appears to bear no malice toward us primates. The harbor seal is a friendly fellow, ever ready to forgive and forget. I was thinking that May morning as we approached Robinson's Rock that, if I wanted to get to know harbor seals better, perhaps I could find one of the species who had no objection to getting to know me better.

Just a few hours before low-water slack we throttled down and began circling the ledge. This is a quiet time in the bay. A string of eider ducks flashed by, making for the mussel beds bared by the ebbing tide. A cormorant—"shag" to Maine coastal people—was perched on the spindle, craning its snakelike neck warily as the boat approached.

Suddenly Bob shoved his thumb over the port bow. "Hey, there's one over there."

I saw the small, sleek head fifty feet dead ahead, only its dome and round eyes above water. Then the seal pup raised his head as if to get a better view. The eyes that met mine showed no alarm.

I took up my net and motioned to Bob to ease the boat forward. I looked around for the pup's mother. No sign of her, and this was odd. Seal mothers are extremely protective of their newborn.

Then a curious and totally unexpected thing happened. Instead of submerging, the pup swam directly toward the boat. I swooped down with my net and swung the little orphan inboard.

Of course, I'll never know for certain that Andre was an

orphan. The fact that the pup was unattended made this a reasonable assumption. Normally, a seal mother has but one pup. On those rather rare occasions when two are whelped, one is usually abandoned. This suggests that the female seal doesn't possess the mammary equipment to care adequately for a pair.

The lot of an abandoned pup is slow starvation or sudden death by the teeth of a great white shark—in Maine, the harbor seal's sole enemy other than man.

It would be sentimentalizing to suggest that Andre showed gratitude at his deliverance. A two-day-old seal has no more capacity for anything beyond the most primitive emotions than a two-day-old child. Nonetheless, there was something different about this little fellow from the start.

Thrust suddenly into a new and strange situation and confronted by creatures whose size alone poses a threat, a wild thing normally will react with hostility, either active or cowering. Not so with Andre. He proceeded to make himself at home. He went bellying about the boat, examining every nook and cranny, curious and playful as a domestic kitten.

In my honest opinion, only its mother sees a newborn human child as a thing of beauty. A two-day-old seal is truly beautiful. Lank as a salamander, its pelt smooth as a grape, the seal pup is an almost perfect miniature of its destined maturity. Streamlined as a teardrop, its power sheathed tightly to move in the watery wildness without a murmur, the harbor seal is a marvel of engineering.

I reached down and patted the satiny head. "Hello there, little fellow," I said.

The soft eyes that met mine were completely trusting. Without realizing it, I made a commitment that day fifteen years ago. There was no way of knowing at the time that Andre might be with me for life, his or mine.

My wife, Thalice, and I were bringing up five children that spring. The children are now, all but one, out of the nest and married. Not only has seal Andre refused to run off and get married, but he has steadfastly and of his own free choice passed up the opportunity to return to the wild.

Wild creatures have been tamed and trained by man before and since, but never before, so far as I am aware, has such a relationship been established in the wild creature's natural habitat and continued over so long a period. That tiny 19-pound seal pup is now a 240-pound elder citizen, an old friend, companion, and, to some degree, dependent. There is little I could do about that even if I wished to.

Why did I want a seal for a friend and companion? I've been asked that question, and I've asked it of myself. The easy answer is: Why *not* a seal? I've heard of people who have made pets of cobras and black widow spiders. Presumably, they found them interesting.

I wish I could say that having a seal was a childhood dream— that at the age of six, a harbor seal was at the top of my Christmas list for Santa. But I suspect I asked for the usual bike or fire engine.

So I have no satisfying answer. I can say that seals have always fascinated me. As a boy hunting in the salt marshes I would see an occasional harbor seal. I recall being stirred one day by the sight of an old bull. He rose up suddenly just beyond the grasses and, droplets glistening on his patriarchal whiskers, bade me a pleasant good morning. I felt a tingling thread of communion running between us. It was my feeling then and later that seals are wise and friendly creatures. I had the curious sense that they wished to be friends.

In the case of Andre, this wish has come to pass. Even as I changed a wild seal's life by deliverance, so he changed mine. Certainly, life has not been the same for either of us since.

Harry with baby seals. (Jim Moore)

2

As the Twig Is Bent

From the time I was aware of the world around me I have felt a kinship with wild creatures. I was brought up close by the great salt marshes that lay seaward of my early home in Salisbury, Massachusetts. These wild tidal meadows abounded with an incredible variety of life. They were the home of rabbit, raccoon, rail, black duck, and heron. Here, the bittern nested and the marsh hawk hunted. I lived in a white frame house in the village, but my true home was this windswept wilderness of grass.

My father's forebears came to this region from England before the American Revolution. My mother was Swedish. Her family went west and settled in Minnesota. So my people on both sides were pioneers, and from way back they were hunters.

The tradition of hunting has deep roots in New England culture; the lore and the love of hunting are passed on from father to son. To this day in rural New England a boy looks eagerly forward to the time when he may legally go afield with a gun.

I was the youngest of a brood of nine—five boys and four girls. When my brothers went out to hunt in the fall, I was forced to curb my impatience. My father, a stern man and strict disciplinarian, was a firm respecter of the law. "When you're fifteen, I'll buy you a hunting license, and not before," he told me.

Unarmed, I roamed the woods and marshes. The youngest in a large and active family is bound to feel a certain amount of isolation. Quite early I fell back on the companionship of nonhuman creatures, winged and footed. Among my close associates was a pair of geese that followed me to school, "which," as the nursery rhyme puts it, "was against the rule."

My first wild pets were crows. I had a pal named Klinker who came along on crow-napping expeditions. The tree man I was to be was foreshadowed early. Always the one who climbed the tree to raid the nests, I learned from experience that when a baby crow responds to intrusion by opening its mouth for food, you have a trainable bird. If it bites your finger, forget it. I also learned that a juvenile crow already feathered out under its wings is too old to domesticate successfully.

It was on one of these crowing expeditions that, quite by accident, I came upon a squirrels' nest. Spotting this cache of leaves high in a tree, I shinnied up to investigate, and I uncovered a litter of newborn gray squirrels. Every bit as startled as I, the tiny creatures tumbled to the ground.

I yelled to Klinker, "Latch onto them!"

This he did, getting nipped a few times in the process. He managed to capture three. After packing them in grass in my lunch box, we headed for home in triumph.

I expect all parents have heard the question "Can I keep them?" Fortunately my father had a soft spot for gray squirrels. He allowed that maybe I could. He went farther than that; he agreed to build a squirrel house if I would take care of them.

I didn't have the foggiest notion of how to go about bringing up unweaned gray squirrels. I assumed they would lap up milk from a saucer like kittens, but my helpless charges refused to cooperate.

Finally, I had an inspiration. Squirrels are rodents. If they wouldn't lap, they might gnaw. I soaked a coarse dishrag in milk and offered it in a dish. The half-starved little fellows went right at it.

Tom, Dick, and Harry, as they were dubbed, thrived. My father spent all day Sunday building a house for them, and Klinker and I brought in a small tree and set it up inside the enclosure to make them feel at home. Everyone was delighted, including the squirrels.

As is true of many idyllic relationships, this one was short-lived. No sooner had my pets become adjusted to their controlled environment than my law-and-order father said to himself, "Hmm, that boy is keeping wild squirrels in captivity. There must be a law against that."

He was right, as a call to the local game warden proved. "What you need is a permit," the warden told my father. "It'll cost you ten dollars."

"That's it," my father said to me. "Let those squirrels loose."

I will never know if my father's edict was prompted by fear of the law or his respect for ten dollars. Both of us choking back tears, my friend and I bade farewell to our bushy-tailed pets.

The leave-taking ceremony proved to be premature. Tom, Dick, and Harry refused to take to the woods. They decided to hang around where the living was easy. I made it even easier by cutting a hole in the kitchen's screen door. The frisky freeloaders would poke their heads through the hole for a dole of peanuts or stale doughnuts that I just happened to have put by.

My father caught on to that soon enough. When he shut off the food supply, Tom, Dick, and Harry simply went on town welfare. They took to hanging around the bus stop across the square. The waiting passengers would buy crackers in the store and feed the little beggars. There were no complaints until the canny rascals, observing the source of the goodies, began raiding the store. The irate storekeeper threatened to sue my father. Dad's weakness for gray squirrels had by this time cooled somewhat. He threatened to shoot them.

I had nightmarish visions of Tom, Dick, and Harry ending up in a squirrel pie. They saved me the anguish. One day in the fall, they went off into the woods and never returned. In hindsight, I have the suspicion that one of the trio should have been called Gertrude, and Gertrude had had something more important than petty larceny on her mind.

Came that great day when I turned fifteen. As good as his word, my father presented me with a gunning license. From that moment on, until it came time for me to go away to school, I haunted the marshes and the woods. The season opened with snipe and ended in the spring with rabbits. In between, there were ducks, geese, and pheasants for quarry. I was a hunter, and a good one.

Those who have never hunted are inclined to see the gunner in the villain's role. Having been raised in the tradition of hunting, I have never felt the need to defend my early bent. A successful hunter must be a good naturalist and a keen observer. What I learned as a kid about nature's realm I could have learned only as a hunter. More important, I acquired a profound respect for wild creatures. Once this respect grows into a deep feeling of kinship, the hunter may, as I have, lay his gun aside. I am not a "reformed" hunter; as a personal matter, I simply choose not to hunt.

It was during this period of my mid-teens that I acquired a set of live decoys. "Call ducks," as they were termed, were legal when I was a boy. The use of these "Judas" ducks to toll in their wild brothers was outlawed in the mid-1930s.

Call ducks were the bread and butter of the old market hunters, whose trade had been banned for some time. There were still a number of these old market hunters around who enjoyed talking about the "good old days." It was from these professional hunters that I learned the fine art of selecting a set of call ducks.

These old pros used a half-dozen or more live callers. Because I rode to the marshes on a bike, I decided three were about all I could handle. I spent a part of one summer visiting backcountry farmers who kept mallard flocks. I'd take a duck aside and listen to its call. What I wanted was one duck with a single call and another with a double call. I needed one drake, but his call didn't matter too much so long as he could make a drake call and wasn't loose-mouthed and foolish.

Finally I found a set of callers that satisfied me and negotiated for them. It took me some weeks to choose and orchestrate that team of call ducks, but when I was finished I had one of the best around.

Once the law was off ducks, away I'd go on my bike in the predawn laden down with my gun and live callers. I had a booth on the marsh—what would be called a blind today. I'd tether one duck on the water to the right within gunshot range and the other to the left. The drake would be tethered behind the blind.

Waiting for the first light, I would hear the call ducks dabbling and preening. Occasionally one of them, feeling lonely, would quack and a sister would answer. The drake would never fail to acknowledge the exchange with his own asthmatic quack.

In the predawn blackness, I'd hear that stirring sound of wings. These were black duck mostly, the smartest and shyest of all waterfowl. The captive callers would respond, the single caller to the right and the double caller to the left. The drake would add his welcoming quack. If the chorus sounded reassuring, the wild blacks would jack in.

The professional hunters had briefed me well. "Don't be impatient, boy," they told me. "Wait until you can see to shoot, and wait until them ducks are bunched up good. Then aim for one in the center of the raft. When the ducks jump, shoot what you can in the air."

I got my share of ducks that way. My pleasure in hunting was enhanced by my father's appreciation of the free bounty. During those Depression years, you may be sure that nothing was wasted.

The fall I went away to school I left my call ducks with a farmer friend, who reported when I returned in the spring that a great horned owl, one moonlit night, had gotten them—every one.

There were dogs in my early life, of course. From the time I was six I had a burning desire to own a dog, a passion that was unrequited until I was thirteen, for what my father considered sound reasons. Before I came on the scene he had owned a pair of excellent rabbit hounds. He was convinced that no other dogs could match them, and he didn't want another dog around the place that would suffer by comparison.

However, my oldest brother, Loring, had a mind of his own, and one day brought home a hound pup. He told me to keep my hands off the dog. Loring would leave the pup in his pen while he went off to work each day. He named the dog Dick. As soon as Loring went off to work I'd go to the pen and talk to Dick, almost crying because I couldn't let him loose and play with him. Finally, Loring softened up. He said he didn't have time to exercise the pup properly. Maybe it would be all right if I took him into the woods each day for some work. That was an unforgettable moment for me. It wasn't long before Loring told me the dog was mine. Dick and I became inseparable.

I was too young to hunt, but together we prepared for the day I could. I devoted a year and a half to training him in the field, and by the time I was old enough to get a license, Dick was quite a dog. He would hunt squirrels if I asked him to and ignore them when I told him to let them be. He'd work on rabbit, pheasant, duck, or partridge, and never appeared to be confused about what I had in mind. He even learned to retrieve when he saw that I was having trouble locating the downed game.

For three wonderful years Dick and I hunted every legal day. After school, the bus would drop me off at my front door and there would be Dick waiting for me. No one had to worry about his running off; this was an appointment Dick didn't want to miss. But the end of these carefree days came abruptly. I graduated from high school in June of 1933, excited by the alluring prospect of a fall devoted exclusively to hunting. But a fall afield wasn't in the cards. My father was the local postmaster, and when he took sick I had to step in and take over the job. In those days, a postmaster worked ten hours a day and six days a week, so what little hunting I got in was in the early morning hours before work.

My father died in December of that year, and the government contract ran out in February. Out of a job, I was restive after having been cooped up in that post office so long. When my mother suggested that I go out to Minnesota to visit her brother Albert, I jumped at the chance.

Uncle Albert was a mythic man to me. He had staked out a claim in that Minnesota wilderness in 1900, and alone he had made himself what to my young mind was a perfect life. He would write to my mother occasionally, and she would tell me tantalizing bits about Uncle Albert's life in his wild paradise. He would write such things as "Saw a timber wolf cross the lake last night," or "It's sixty below zero outdoors—too cold for even the grindstone to be out." At age nineteen this was rich and heady stuff. I left home in March with twenty dollars in my pocket, a pack on my back, and I thumbed my way west.

The reality I found when I arrived was as good as the dream. Game was plentiful, and there was no closed season—or if there was, it was never brought to my attention. I lived on venison, prairie chicken, grouse, and duck. There were wolves, bears, and bobcats in the brush, but I shot only what I could eat, and no more than I could eat. Except for fish, Uncle Albert was a vegetarian, so I was left to forage for myself.

My strongest remembrance is of the stillness. My cousin Hugh Shogren lived downriver about five miles from Uncle Albert's clearing. I was impressed by Hugh's ability to hear a car traveling down the nearest road three miles off, but soon in that stillness I could do the same.

Uncle Albert seemed to be happy leading, as he did, a hand-to-mouth existence. He owned one cow, and his dairy equipment consisted of one hand-run cream separator. As soon as he could accumulate five gallons of cream, he would tote them two miles and leave them standing against his mailbox to be picked up whenever the buyer happened by. The buyer would leave the money in the mailbox. Thus Uncle Albert would get cash to purchase such things as pipe tobacco, sugar, salt, coffee, and the few other items he couldn't grow or make himself.

The lake on which his cabin stood was called Rice Lake, and well named it was. It had the appearance of a huge grain field, the stalks standing three to four feet above the water. Wild ducks came there by the thousands to stuff themselves on rice every day. Several pairs of Ojibwa Indians would also appear to gather the rice. Their method was this: One man paddled the canoe, and another man, sitting amidships, would bend the stalks over the canoe with a stick and would then hit that stick with another stick, and the rice would fall into the canoe. After they had enough for themselves, they would get extra and trade it to Albert for vegetables. Albert was an excellent cook, and I enjoyed his wild-rice puddings topped off with thick fresh cream from old Bossy. Another of his dishes was buckwheat pancakes, topped off with his own thick cream and his homemade butter.

My cousin Hugh occasionally visited us while I was there. We hunted together, and one day we got a small deer. We gave all but a hind leg to Hugh's family and headed back to Uncle Albert's. Uncle Albert would have none of it, but encouraged Hugh and me to cook and eat it. We decided to have venison steak smothered in onions. We could find only one onion in the bin, so I explained to Uncle Albert that we wanted to smother the steak. He didn't understand that particular term, but he agreed to get some more from the garden. Returning with only two onions, he remarked, "There! These should be enough to smother anything." We needed about six, but we didn't have the guts to tell him, so we made do. The dish turned out fine.

Every second year, Uncle Albert would cut enough wood to last two years. The summer that I was there was an off year, so the woodshed was full of neatly stacked firewood. He had, besides the hardwood, about a half cord of cedar and an enormous bin full of birch bark. He showed me how to get a cooking fire going almost as fast as with today's electric range by using birch bark, finely split sticks of cedar, and firewood, in that order.

Uncle Albert liked his grounds to be neat and well kept. He always had a flower garden. However, he confided in me that his lawn hadn't been mowed for years previous to my visit because of his advancing age and gradually failing health. I took the hint and said, "Too bad you don't have a lawn mower, because I could do it for you." He replied that he had one that was pretty well shot, but that he would repair it. My heart sank, because at this point the grass had gone rank and tall. He repaired the mower, so I worked to the point of exhaustion mowing and raking and removing until I had a space that was quite presentable. The space was fifty by a hundred feet, in front of the cabin and around the flower bed.

Uncle Albert had been away during my labor, so when he came back I said, "Well, there it is." He said, "Well done, my boy, but you know, when I used to mow it, I kept it cut from way down by the barn to about equal distance the other way." This was at least three-quarters of an acre. Well, I did it, and kept it mowed all summer. It was worth it to me because he seemed so pleased. But I almost fell out of favor with him on one occasion. I was sitting in the main room of the cabin and he came in with a large bunch of gorgeous flowers. I said, "Wow, what beautiful roses!" He stopped dead in his tracks and replied, "You idiot, these are peonies!" But he laughed it off with a curt "You don't know much about flowers, do you?"

My botanical ignorance gave Uncle Albert considerable satisfaction. The first week I was there he had said to me, "Boy, you shoot anything you want, but leave my songbirds be." Before a week was out, I was pointing out to Uncle Albert varieties of songbirds he didn't know existed. He was also surprised at my hunting prowess, having the mistaken notion that any lad from the East was bound to be a greenhorn in the woods.

As I said, I killed only what I needed to eat, which left a good deal of time for simply observing the natural world. I spent a part of the early summer watching a pair of blue-winged teal bringing up their young. I checked the nest each day from eggs to fledglings. The mother, fiercely alarmed at first, soon got used to my presence and permitted me to watch her activities at close range.

One afternoon Uncle Albert, Hugh, and I were outside, cleaning new potatoes that my uncle had just dug. In a rare talkative mood, he commenced to tell Hugh and me the story of how he had decided to settle in that particular spot, and we were hypnotized. It seems that in his late thirties he had developed chronic appendicitis and been advised to start a new life. His trade had been that of maintenance man for various logging companies, and he knew of government land that was available in northern Minnesota. With map and compass he traveled north from St. Paul to Northhome, Minnesota, to look for a certain "40" that someone had told him about.

In his own words: "I looked and looked for that particular spot, but I just wasn't woodsman enough to find it. One day I met a man who told me about this place here as being available. I came down, took one look, and knew that this was for me." Then he went on to tell about going back to St. Paul for his tools and cookstove.

He came to Deer River by team and then decided to go the rest of the way by duck boat, a small double-ended contraption that could be rowed. Outside of hard work, the trip was uneventful until he came to Rice Lake, on the opposite side from his cabin. He ran into a heavy windstorm and had visions of losing tools, stove, and everything else. He had no bailing can and the waves were coming over the side, so he took off one shoe and used it to bail with. He made it, but he still shuddered when he told about it.

Then came the work of felling the trees and cutting them into boards, timbers, framing, and so forth—all done by hand. Using an adz and a one-man crosscut saw, he dovetailed the corners as smooth as any cabinetmaker's joints. The roof and floorboards he cut from virgin white pine by pit-sawing the logs, some of which were twenty-four inches wide and at least twenty feet long, without a knot in their entire length.

Uncle Albert's tolerance of the wild creatures around him did not extend to woodchucks and crows that raided his garden. I got rid of his woodchucks and pocketed the ten cents each they brought in bounty. At first he was wrathy when instead of shooting crows, I tamed one of them. He quickly got over his prejudice.

The crow, named Columbus, would come from a half-mile off when I whistled. He finally took up residence in the woodshed and accompanied me on walks, perched on my shoulder. The wild crows didn't think much of Columbus's apostasy and would set up an awful fuss. Columbus ignored them.

When the time approached for me to leave, Uncle Albert said, "Now, you be sure to take that crow with you when you go."

I couldn't see myself traveling cross-country a thousand miles with a crow on my shoulder. I had no intention of taking Columbus home with me, and I guess Uncle Albert knew it.

When the day came, I shook hands with the old man and started off on the ten-mile hike to the highway. "Just a minute, boy," Uncle Albert said. "You forgot that crow."

I tried to appear surprised. "Well, so I did!" There was nothing I could do but whistle for Columbus and start off with a crow on my shoulder.

Once I was five miles down the trail I said good-bye to Columbus, a farewell that didn't take at once. He followed me for a few miles, hopping from tree to tree. Finally, he went out of my life forever.

When I heard sometime later that he had been shot by a farmer who didn't know he was tame, I regretted not taking him east.

It occurred to me too late that he would have been an asset. A young fellow with a pack on his back and a crow on his shoulder would have stopped cars in their tracks and simplified his hitchhike home.

In November of that year I received word that Uncle Albert had died at the age of seventy-five. I went back in September of 1966 to look the old place over. Both the barn and the cabin had collapsed, but surprisingly, the garden area had not become overgrown with trees. The wild rice was gone from the lake, but civilization had done little to change this boyhood paradise.

Andre made himself at home in the Goodridge house (Goodridge Collection)

And stairs didn't deter Andre from entering the house. (Camden Herald*)*

3

A Family Affair

It is a far journey in time and space from that cabin in the Minnesota wilds, where I ran free as a hare, to a home in a Maine coastal village filled with a wife and a brood of growing children. The span can be compassed quickly: two years of forestry training at the New York State Ranger School, marriage, four and a half years in the army during World War II, eighteen months of which were spent at a Radio Intelligence outpost in Iceland, and, finally, the establishment of the Goodridge Tree Service in Rockport, Maine. Starting a family, though important enough for the record, was just standard procedure.

At the time of Andre's arrival our children ranged in age from seven to nineteen. My mother once said of a self-satisfied neighbor who couldn't resist praising up her children that she thought all her geese were swans. I'll only say that I hope the kids are as pleased with me as I am with them. Since my office has always been in the house, they've seen more of me than most children see of their fathers. I like to think that having me underfoot over the years has been educational; they have learned to expect anything.

Certainly the advent of a two-day-old seal didn't dismay them. In those years, life in the Goodridge family was one adopted animal after another; the children thought living in a zoo was perfectly normal.

The oldest of the children are the twins, Steve and Susan. Steve was the woodsman. He went with me into the woods as soon as he could walk. Later he joined me in scuba diving and quickly became expert at it. Sue was a true animal lover. She vowed when she was twelve that she'd forsake marriage and become an old maid veterinarian, a vow she kept only until she met Ken Crane, a fellow student at the University of Maine.

Carol, who was seventeen at the time of Andre's coming, was more studious than the others. The pet robin could land on her head while she was in a book and she'd scarcely notice the intrusion. Nonetheless, Carol was softhearted about animals. She was the one who would get up in the night to let a dog or a cat out, or go forth in the dark to see what was wrong with Mrs. Cluck-Cluck, a fat old Rhode Island Red who for a time ruled the roost.

Paula, four years younger than Carol, preferred chickens to dolls. In fact, all the girls at that certain age substituted live creatures for the usual store-bought babies. It was Toni, the youngest, whose idea it was that rooster Jake and Mrs. Cluck-Cluck should have a marriage ceremony. After all, they'd been going together for a number of years. One afternoon down by the pond the nuptials were duly solemnized, Mrs. Cluck-Cluck dressed fit to kill in a white gown and train, a hole conveniently cut to allow for her tail.

There were the usual mice, snakes, frogs, and spiders. Steve, who was to become a civil engineer, was more practical than his sisters. At the sandbox age he liked his insects to be useful. He came into the house one day quite pleased with himself.

"I've been giving ants a ride," he said. "They had fun."

What he'd done, I soon learned, was capture a dragonfly and

load it down with ants. Thus loaded with passengers, the dragonfly was made airborne. I'm not at all sure the dragonfly enjoyed itself.

Later, Steve took over the autopsies when occasions arose. There was the time a raccoon got George, a gaudy and personable bantam rooster. The girls spotted what they assumed was the culprit in a tree in a nearby copse. I shot the coon and Steve performed the autopsy. At least he began the operation. Paula, though fascinated, kept uttering expressions of disgust. After warning her to keep quiet, Steve flipped the knife into the ground and walked off. Without hesitation, Sue stepped in and took over.

The feathers that were found in the coon's stomach constituted presumptive evidence of guilt. Thalice cooked the coon liver for lunch. All the kids ate the liver, but only Carol found it delicious. She said it tasted like chicken.

Over the years there was a series of pet fowl, the most memorable of which were Inez, Blanche, and Madeline. They had their own quarters, but they wandered at will into the house when they found a door inadvertently left open.

Though the children were the official guardians of the chickens, I was the one they came to for succor. If a strange dog happened to wander into the yard, they'd come flying into the house and land in my lap. Our own dogs were their friends, of course. In fact, Madeline often slept in the doghouse with Dick, my first beagle, and invariably laid her eggs there. Madeline was George's consort. When George met his untimely end, Madeline adopted Dick and the two became inseparable.

There was a pigeon, inevitably named Walter. As a fledgling, he'd fallen out of the nest under the highway bridge that spans Goose River. I built a cote for him and trained him to return to it. Walter was a common, garden variety town pigeon, but he was quite a homer. I'd take him as far as six miles off, release him, and try to beat him home. I'd have to drive well over thirty miles an hour to win the race.

Walter spent a good deal of his time down at the pond with the ducks. Because he ignored other town pigeons, I have an idea he thought he was a duck. Moreover, he considered himself the boss duck. When he didn't like the way the ducks behaved, he'd discipline them until they shaped up.

We also had a pet seagull who was quite a tyrant. A friend found him wounded at the town dump and brought him to me. Once his wing had healed he could have flown off, but he preferred to stay around to be hand-fed and to bully the barnyard. Dick was scared to death of him, and Sam Segal, as he was known, served to confirm what I'd heard about seagulls: They will eat anything. One day, I fed him some canned sardines on a clothespin. He ate the sardines, clothespin and all, with no apparent ill effects.

Toni, the baby of the tribe, was a wizard at catching songbirds. She'd talk to them, gentle them, and let them go. I said to her one day, "Those little songbirds you catch must be pretty stupid. You catch a boat-tailed grackle and you've done something."

Within a half-hour, Toni was back with a boat-tailed grackle.

"You mean one of these?" she asked.

Thalice, though at times sorely tried, has been patient over the years. Her early conditioning may account for her tolerance. Her Maine Yankee father, True Spear, ran a rather loose ship. True was a man of many trades and as unpredictable as a dollar cuckoo clock. He would quote long passages from Shakespeare at the breakfast table. He devoted his spare time, and some that wasn't so spare, to inventing gadgets that people could get along without.

Among her father's more memorable inventions was an electric rat trap. He was an electrical genius himself, and the only problem with the trap was that the user needed to be, if not a genius, a better than average engineer. And in the days before central heating, he eliminated the distasteful chore of getting up in a cold house to light the stove by rigging up a Rube Goldberg contraption that lighted the fire when the alarm went off while he remained cozily in bed.

In short, living in an odd household was nothing new to Thalice. And she had long since ceased being concerned about what the neighbors thought. I'm sure there must have been talk about little Toni going about with a diapered pet hen in her doll carriage instead of the usual baby doll.

One neighbor was a bit uneasy when she heard from the children that I was building a bat cage. "Has he got any bats?" the neighbor asked Thalice one winter day. Thalice thought it best to quiet her fears. "Only the ones he has in his belfry," she said.

Fortunately, the lady never did learn what a close call we all had. I was indeed interested in bats at that time, and not at all surprised when a small friend of Toni's brought me a bat one day. Neighborhood children were forever bringing into the Goodridge household creatures they didn't dare take home.

I found the bat a most fascinating creature. He would come to me each night and crawl up my arm, pulling himself along by his wings. He would take flies from my hand and eat them with relish. He devoured moths too, spitting out the wings. He permitted me to hold him and seemed to enjoy being petted.

Paula, my second youngest, was horrified. She threatened to move out of the house. The crisis was averted. The bat adventure ended abruptly, but not before I'd satisfied myself that a bat is both tamable and trainable.

It was with the idea of supporting this hunch that one night in deep winter I went to an abandoned quarry where I knew bats were hibernating. The quarry was frozen over, and it was necessary to cross thin ice to the far wall of the open cave. I wore my scuba wet suit, in case I broke through; nonetheless, it was quite a spooky experience crossing the ice and crawling into that black cave. I found the dormant bats in the old dynamite drill holes. With the aid of a flashlight I poked a few out and brought them home.

I secreted the bats in the cellar and, while I waited for them to come out of their winter's sleep, I started on that bat cage. Early in March, Operation Bat was suddenly aborted.

What happened was that Thalice, somewhat concerned, decided to do some research on her own. She phoned the local vet, "Mac" McDonald.

A word about Mac is in order here. Mac, now gone, was to play a small but important role in my seal adventures. He was a genial and obliging fellow, and well learned in his profession. He lived on a backcountry road. He was sometimes difficult to locate, but nothing was too much trouble for Mac if an animal was involved. He was a special friend of my children's. Toni brought him a mouse with a broken leg one day and asked him to put a splint on it. And then there was Beulah, the guinea pig, who sustained a double hernia when a strange dog chased her, and required Mac's professional attention. Mac's patience was inexhaustible; his tolerance, majestic. If you paid Mac for his services, he'd accept the money, but he never seemed to get around to sending out bills. I don't think he ever kept books.

My favorite story about Mac concerns his kennel man, Chick. Chick loved to hunt woodcock and kept a good bird dog. One fine fall day, Chick didn't show up at nine. Mac asked a lady who'd come with a cat if she'd wait until he checked on Chick, who lived up the road a short piece. "He may be sick," he told the lady.

Mac knocked on Chick's door in vain. Then he noted that the

doghouse was empty. The lady with the cat gave Mac a questioning look when he arrived back at the office. "The dog's gone, too. Guess they're both sick," Mac told her.

When Thalice called Mac to ask if there were hazards involved in this bat business, Mac's reply was quick and unequivocal. "Don't know any more hazardous business, unless it's sorting bobcats. Tell him to lay off."

Mac went on to say that if you checked a hundred dogs for rabies and found four positive, that would be a high percentage. "Check a hundred bats and the chances are, you'll find about forty-five rabid."

That was that. The bats went.

The flying squirrel that joined our household was a more engaging guest, and considerably more acceptable to all concerned. My crew was taking down an old tree one day when a pair of flying squirrels tumbled out of a cavity. I appropriated one of them with the idea of showing it to the kids and then releasing it. These nocturnal, gliding cousins of the gray squirrel are common enough, but they are rarely seen, because they don't appear, willingly at least, in the daylight hours.

Since Charlie, as he was dubbed, was mature, I doubted that he could be tamed. I was wrong about that. He adopted his new home without the slightest trauma. We learned quickly that he loved apples, and he'd eat them right out of our hands. We gave him the freedom of the house. We never did learn where he slept during the day. Each evening, promptly at dusk, he would appear. He'd come gliding out from some place and join us for supper. He was always free to leave our bed and board, and this he did one evening. He simply glided out the door and disappeared.

And then there was Reuben, the insatiable robin. Steve,

returning from school one day, found the fledgling on the ground. He located the nest and put him back where he belonged. Again he tumbled out. So Steve brought him home. What else?

We'd gather night crawlers from the lawn to feed Reuben. He couldn't get enough of them. He must have eaten his weight in worms at each sitting, and still wanted more.

For reasons I've never fathomed, many wild creatures are fascinated by splashing water. Reuben would fly into the bathroom while the children took their Saturday-night baths. He'd sit on the toilet seat, enthralled, while the kids played in the tub water. Reuben was no great help to Thalice when she was doing the dishes. He'd insist on sitting on the lip of the dishpan. One day, he fell into the soapy water. He emerged covered with suds and not a bit subdued by the experience.

There were a few problems, certainly. A caller who didn't know the family too well would be startled, understandably, when a robin landed on his head. And, needless to say, a housebound robin that ate his weight in worms was in constant need of maid service.

A robin is a feisty bird. He won't take anything from anybody. Coming into the house one day, I accidentally kicked Reuben. He went at me, beak and talon. I told him I was sorry. He made up with me after a day or so.

Reuben remained in the neighborhood all that summer. He came to my whistle from wherever he was and sat on my shoulder to be fed. When the robins gathered in the fall, preparatory to heading south, he joined the flock, no better—and, we hoped, no worse—for his association with the Goodridges.

As the breadwinner, I expect I am nominally the head of the house. In practical terms, I discovered early that the democratic process has something to be said for it. To some people, all creatures of a species are alike. But it requires only a brief association with wild things to realize that no duplicates exist in nature; no two blades of grass or peas in a pod are alike. Certainly, the members of the Goodridge family are as dissimilar as people can be.

As our children all had names, so did our feral wards. A name is an acknowledgment of individuality. Reuben was a bird; he was also a robin; and, more specifically and meaningfully, he was Reuben.

The problem, of course, was how to agree on a name. Each Goodridge had his own idea of a proper moniker. The one-man, one-vote principle resolved that situation. On these baptismal occasions, each member of the family wrote a name on a ballot and tossed it into the hat. Originally, our thought was to have the creature pick its own name out. That didn't work out. The first arbiter, a squirrel, ate his chosen name before we could see it. We ended up with the youngest making the draw.

The democratic process brought peace to the family. It also produced some pretty weird names: a guinea pig named Queen Elizabeth, a squirrel named Apple Pie.

We had more adopted squirrels than anything else over the years. Gray squirrels have enjoyed a long association with man, and are the easiest of all wild animals to tame. They are very self-sufficient as well. We'd put out a box of facial tissues. The squirrels would take what they needed to build their nests and settle in, most often in the clothespin bag that hung behind the kitchen door.

During one period I had a beagle named Toot who assumed a supervisory role in our complicated household. He was as patient as an English nanny, and his tolerance was monumental. Bugs, one of our pet rabbits, got bored easily. Aware, perhaps, that beagles were supposed to chase rabbits, he insisted that Toot chase him. It didn't matter that Toot might be sleeping peacefully in the sun. Bugs would keep nudging Toot until, reluctantly, he obliged and gave Bugs a quick romp around the yard.

Toot was also a big help when Toni's guinea pig, Beulah, got lost, which she did about once a week. Beulah wasn't too bright. She'd wander off and none of us could find her. I'd call Toot and tell him, "Go get Beulah!" Dutifully, Toot would track her down and shepherd her home, baying on her trail until she was safely in her pen.

There was, of course, a horse. At a certain age, every girl wants a horse. Toni had Tiffany, and Tiffany was every bit as obliging and tractable as Toot. I admit to a weakness for practical jokes. I have a neighbor named Eben, who to my knowledge has never refused a drink. Tiffany would follow Toni anywhere, even into the kitchen. When I found Tiffany in the kitchen one day, I had an idea that was too good to waste.

One afternoon in the Christmas season, I got Toni to lead Tiffany into the kitchen. I called Eben to come over and have a drink with me. We sat in my office off the kitchen. After Eben had lifted a few and was feeling no pain, I pushed open the kitchen door. There was Tiffany eyeing Eben blandly as if to say, "So what else is new?"

Eben shook his head a few times and blinked. "That looks like a horse in the kitchen," Eben said. He went home shortly. I can't say he took the pledge, but it did slow him up a bit.

There's a little more to the story. Not wanting to risk leading Tiffany down the narrow stone steps that led from the kitchen, we decided to let her out the front door, where the steps were wider and more shallow. As Tiffany was making her exit, I heard the squeal of brakes. Our neighbor Mrs. Locke, en route home, had narrowly missed running into our hedge.

A few moments later the phone rang. It was Mrs. Locke. She

had just come home from a Christmas party, she said. Then a pause. "I thought I saw a horse come out your front door as I came by."

Mrs. Locke was a very nice lady, and certainly most temperate in her habits. I should have told her that as a matter of fact, a horse had come out the front door of the Goodridge residence. The incorrigible imp in me was not so kind.

"Did you indeed, Mrs. Locke?" was all I said.

4

Marky and Basil

Mothers are fond of saying that the first child is the hardest. As a substitute mother I can echo that observation. I would not have succeeded with Andre without the knowledge I had gained from my first two seals, Marky and Basil.

Natural mothers prepare physically and emotionally for the experience of motherhood. Lacking that advantage, I became an instant mother. I was not taken completely by surprise, of course. I had only to remember my childhood experiences with wild birds and animals to realize that creatures separated early from their mothers and adopted by man have difficulty in identifying with their own kind. I'd learned that with my pet crows and squirrels. And certainly Mary learned that with her little lamb.

So far as those first two seal pups were concerned, I was their mother. I had all the best intentions in the world, but what I didn't realize at the time was the depth of my innocence. I was not, as they say, a fit mother.

I was hunting sharks that summer of 1959. I admit to an antipathy for sharks in general, and the great white, or man-eater, shark in particular. Intellectually, I'm satisfied that everything has its place in the marine ecosystem; there is nothing "good" or "bad" in nature's terms. Nonetheless, I can't abide these mindless machines of destruction. Call it a human prejudice.

I had another and possibly no more admirable reason for harpooning great white sharks: I hoped to prove that certain marine biologists were in error. I expect that most of us amateur naturalists delight in finding the scientific establishment wrong. All too often those lab–bound fellows concern themselves with analytical and statistical data and ignore the raw material of life. Relying on their brains, they sometimes forget to use their eyes.

A few years ago, I heard about a weather-station man who prepared a fair-weather report based on the panel of instruments in front of him. One look out of the window could have told him that it was snowing like crazy.

Certain highly qualified biologists had suggested that the Gulf of Maine was no more than a "casual range" of the great white shark. I'd harpooned a dozen or more in Penobscot Bay in the course of several summers, and had sighted many more. It struck me that the presence of that many man-eaters constituted more than a "casual" population.

One afternoon, I tried to make this point to some government scientists. I'd been hired by the Office of Naval Research to dive for a project in Penobscot Bay set up to determine the rate of sea growth on underwater installations. In the process of working out some equitable rate, I spoke of the risks involved, and mentioned the presence of the great white shark.

The ONR man smiled. "Don't worry," he said. "The great white shark seldom ranges north of Cape Cod. You've certainly never seen one around here."

Straightfaced, I said, "No, sir, I've never seen a great white shark right here." Then I pointed over the bow of the boat. "But I've seen a dozen or more right over there."

I got what *I* considered an equitable rate.

Although the pursuit of great white sharks was a Captain Ahab obsession in those years, making a friend of a harbor seal was becoming more and more my abiding passion. I couldn't quite put down the curious feeling that a harbor seal had something to tell me.

I was down on the waterfront preparing to set out on a shark hunt when Freddie Wilson, a lobsterman who knew of my interest in seals, hailed me.

"Hey, Harry," he said, "just spotted a young seal off Mark Island."

"You sure, Freddie?" I asked.

Freddie snorted. " 'Course I'm sure. Haven't had a drink yet today. Ain't that pitiful?"

I headed out, putting a white mustache at the bow of my boat. I owned at the time a lap-straked nineteen–footer, powered by a 75-horsepower Johnson outboard. She was fast, weatherly, and extreme-ly maneuverable.

If Freddie had had a drink, which was likely, it hadn't impaired his vision. As I came under the lee on Mark Island, I spotted the pup. I had no equipment for capturing seals; in fact, I had no idea what equipment was necessary.

When the sleek little head dropped from sight, I searched the water for a sign of the pup's mother. Even before I enjoyed a close relationship with seals, I felt a reluctance to contend with a wild mother for her young. I confess I didn't look too hard that day. Wanting a seal pup badly, I salved my conscience by rationalizing that the mortality rate among seal pups was extremely high, and I was perhaps performing a service by taking this young seal into pro-tective custody.

Such rationalizations seldom stand up under scrutiny. A few years back, Maine bobcat hunters were fighting to preserve the bounty on bobcats. They insisted that bobcats kill deer, and therefore should be eliminated. Later I learned that many of these cat hunters practiced their own form of conservation: They eschewed the killing of female bobcats, reasoning that if they killed too many of them, soon there would be no cats for their hounds to run.

There was a brief period when I accepted commissions to capture seal pups for aquariums. Once I discovered that none of my rationalizations was sturdy enough to withstand my moral compunctions, I refused a number of lucrative assignments.

I captured Marky that day simply by tiring him in a cat-and-mouse game. I reached down into the water and flopped him into the boat by his hind flippers.

Marky, named Mark for the island from whence he came, was no trouble on the trip back to port. He cried a bit, an appealing sound much like the cry of a juvenile crow, only softer: *Krooh, krooh.* The harbor seal, when mature, doesn't utter the sea lion bark. The harbor seal will snort, snarl, and clear his nostrils like a blowing deer; that is the totality of his vocal repertoire.

Sue was waiting at the house when I arrived with that fifteen-pound gift of the sea. A born mother, Sue took the pup in her arms and comforted him. Marky ceased his crying at once.

The transition from sea home to man's abode was accomplished in a matter of hours. I realized that the pup would have to be fed, but I was woefully unprepared for my maternal role. Earlier, I had dug out all the available material on harbor seals. There was little scientific literature on the subject, and much of what I found turned out to be misinformation. Certainly the suggestion that harbor seals are not trained because they are relatively stupid and untrainable proved to be grossly in error.

The common, or harbor, seal (*Phoca vitulina*) is a fish-eating mammal of the suborder Pinnipedia ("finfooted ones"). Four groups of mammals enter the sea: sea otters, manatees, whales and dolphins, walruses and seals. The manatees, whales, and dolphins are exclusively marine; the others rest and bear their young on land and enter the water mainly in search of food.

Five of the pinnipeds can be found in Gulf of Maine waters. The gray seal, easily recognizable by its greater size and massive head, is a summer transient. The harp seal, hooded seal, and walrus are rare visitors. Only the harbor seal is a year-round resident.

The harbor seal is associated with the unvegetated outer or near-shore ledges, preferring those with gentle slopes that are all but covered at the peak of the tide. These haul-out sites are removed from boat traffic lanes and other potential sources of danger and harassment. Harbor seals return year after year to these sites, a fact attested to by the scores of seal ledges that appear on Maine's coastal maps and charts.

Harbor seals form loosely gregarious herds when hauled out at low and half-tide, becoming solitary when they disperse to fish at high water. There is no reliable source of information on the historical abundance of harbor seals in Maine waters. The Maine Indian prized the harbor seal for its flesh and skin, but it is unlikely that his hunting had a marked effect on the early seal populations. It is estimated that the present Maine population is within the range of 7,000 to 9,000, with the highest concentrations east of Casco Bay.

Although of no great commercial value, harbor seals have been harassed along our coast for generations. Many have been destroyed by fishermen convinced that seals eat too many fish, and that fish are exclusively for people. And despite the fact that lobsters have never been found in a harbor seal's stomach, some Maine lobstermen are inclined to include this pinniped among the causes of the declining lobster stocks.

In 1900, in response to pressures from fishermen, the State

established a bounty on the harbor seal. Town clerks accepted seal noses as evidence of destruction, and paid out one dollar per nose. The Passamaquoddy Indians, living as they were at a subsubsistence level, very nearly eliminated the species from the eastern tip of Maine in a desperate effort to eke out their meager incomes.

Over a period of five years, the State paid out nearly $25,000 in bounty. Investigating what appeared to be a highly inflated figure, the authorities discovered that the canny Indians were practicing conservationists. With a hot iron and a little clever crafting, one seal skin was sufficient to fabricate a dozen or more "noses." The bounty was rescinded in 1905, but the harbor seal remained unprotected until 1972, when the federal Marine Mammal Protection Act was passed.

The harbor seal is a widely distributed species, inhabiting coastal regions over much of the Northern Hemisphere. In Europe, its range extends from Portugal along the Atlantic Coast to northern Norway, and westward around the British Isles, Iceland, and Greenland. On the North American West Coast, harbor seals range from Baja California to Alaska; on the East Coast, their range extends from Baffin Bay southward to a latitude somewhat north of New York.

Much of this I learned later. What I did know at the time was that in the Eastern United States, harbor seals breed only in Maine and adjacent waters. I was also aware that the so-called trained seal of zoos and circuses is actually a sea lion, or eared seal. These cousins of the harbor seal stand erect on their large flippers and are able to rotate their hind flippers forward, giving them fair mobility on land. Harbor seals lack this capability, and in consequence are markedly clumsy on land. In the water the harbor seal is matchless and beautiful to behold.

The little I knew and all the seal lore I managed to acquire in a crash course was of little help in my situation. Curiously, no one had bothered to study this common inhabitant of the world's coastal waters very extensively. There was certainly no Dr. Spock on the care and feeding of baby harbor seals available.

One scientific contact that proved rewarding was with a biologist–scuba diver, Carleton Ray. Ray admitted that he didn't know a great deal about harbor seals, but what he did know, he shared with me. I can't fault him for suggesting that I drop the whole idea of bringing up a seal. It was his experience, he told me, that harbor seals became unfriendly and intractable as they matured. Obviously, he had known harbor seals only in a confined and artificial environment. One clue he did offer proved helpful. He told me that seal's milk was roughly ten times as rich as cow's milk.

This information turned out to be strictly academic. I took unsweetened canned milk and fortified it with egg yolks. I tried every way I could think of to get the formula into young Marky. The hungry pup simply refused to eat.

As I struggled with the dilemma, I recalled my youthful experience with baby squirrels. Having nothing to lose, I soaked a dishrag in the formula. As desperate as I, Marky began to chew on the rag and take nourishment.

My triumph was short-lived. Marky perked up a bit, then languished. One morning I found him dead. Mac performed the autopsy. He found a piece of the dishrag in Marky's stomach.

I think I suffered as much as any mother who realizes that in her rearing of a child she has made some fatal mistake. All that ensuing summer I pondered the tragedy and racked my brain for a solution. I'd come so close to success, and I vowed I'd try once more in the spring to bring up a harbor seal. There had been no time to do more with Marky than teach him a few simple tricks, but his response to my direction satisfied me that a harbor seal could be tamed and trained, and would adapt easily to mankind.

Summer trailed into fall, and I was no nearer an answer to the problem of feeding a baby seal. Then in late October I ran into a bit of luck. Near Ram Island I came upon a female harbor seal that had been killed by rifle fire. Exploring the body, I discovered the obvious reason for my failure. The teats of a mother seal are recessed. The two nipples are set deep in dimples in her belly, encircled in a doughnut of fatty tissue. Common sense should have told me that. Because the seal's movement on land is on her belly, such critical equipment could not protrude; logically, it would be recessed for protection.

Armed with this information, I set about constructing an artificial seal mother—at least the part of a seal mother that was most important to a seal pup. I took a log and hollowed out a recess midway along its length and large enough to receive a bulb syringe. I covered the log with foam neoprene, the material of a scuba diver's wet suit. At the base of the rubbery dimple, I made a hole to expose the syringe tip. I went so far as to get down on my hands and knees and try the rig. It worked.

I was ready to try again.

[section break]

[no para] My log contains this brief note: "Caught Basil May 14, 1960. Mouse Island."

I knew by that spring that if I wanted to take a two- or three-day-old seal, I had a narrow window—a matter of a few days around the middle of May. I began my search in the second week of that month.

It was Saturday. A bank of fog lay offshore, ready to roll in. Sue, who was gung ho on this seal business, said, "I've got a feeling today is the day. Let's go."

"Let's go," I agreed.

The sea was flat calm, ideal for spotting seals. That was all that could be said for that morning. Fog closed in on us before we reached the islands. But Sue was right. This was the day. We spotted the seal pup off Mouse Island. After a brief chase and a bit of maneuvering, Sue netted him.

We were in a gray box with the lid down as we started in. I got a bearing on the Owls Head foghorn and the bell buoy off Indian Island and began feeling my way in. Basil (for bay seal: that's what came up in the draw, and he was stuck with it) wasn't at all cooperative on the ticklish trip home. He snarled and nipped at both of us, but by the time we had him home, he was perfectly content in Sue's arms.

The family gathered when the time came for the crucial test. If this one didn't accept its ersatz mother, my seal investigations were over.

And for a while it looked very much that way. Basil looked over the strange rig, nuzzled it a bit, then backed off. But I could see that the rubbery substance interested him. I heated the dimple with warm water. That did it! Basil explored the surface with his nose, came to the warm target, and went at the rubber nipple, cautiously at first, then with gusto.

Sue yelled. I yelled. We all shouted. You might have thought we'd discovered the law of gravity. Seeing a baby take its first step was nothing compared to this triumph.

Basil thrived on his neoprene mother. I knew that somewhere along the line he'd have to be weaned to fish. Seals were piscivorous, were they not? It didn't occur to me that I'd have to explain this to Basil.

After several weeks passed and he refused to be coaxed from his rubber mother, I knew I was faced with another crisis. Lively enough both on land and in the sea, he wasn't gaining weight. I began to emulsify herring and add the mash to the formula. Basil accepted this adjustment, but he refused to look at a whole raw fish, or even a piece of one. More than that, he snorted his disgust at the very idea, and when I shoved a piece of fish into his mouth, he'd spit it out.

July 4 was a red-letter day in my seal log. The entry read, "Basil eats a fish." But there was much more to it than that. When a month had gone by, and then six weeks, I knew something had to be done about Basil's liquid diet. I guessed the nature of the basic problem. Eating raw fish was a learned matter. The seal mother teaches her pup to catch and eat raw fish, much as a vixen teaches her fox pups to catch and eat field mice. The seal pup watches as its mother goes through this essential process, and then imitates her. The stumper was that I had as much chance of catching and eating raw fish in the open sea as I had of giving mother's milk.

I was sitting around the house with Thalice's young brother, True Spear, on that Fourth of July. Basil and I had just come up from a swim, and the seal was dozing on a mat in the kitchen.

"Look," I said to True, "that seal just has to go on raw fish whether he likes it or not. I'm going to force-feed him, and I may need help."

And force-feed him we did. True held his mouth open. I shoved a fish down his throat and then held his mouth shut until he swallowed. The first time, Basil was outraged. He snorted his displeasure. We tried it again. Basil still protested, but this time not so vociferously. The third time, not only did he fail to complain, he blinked his eyes and seemed to say, "Well, that's not so bad after all." When he began to follow me around the house for more raw fish, I knew he was weaned.

So finally I had brought a harbor seal through the most critical period of his life. I had weaned him and taught him to eat fish. More important, we had come to enjoy each other's company. Together, we drove each day to the waterfront in my car to swim and play in the sea. He stayed close to me underwater, pushing his nose against my faceplate every few minutes, or rubbing his sleek body against my legs. Much like the beagle pups I'd taken into the woods, Basil wanted me in his sight: I represented security in an unfamiliar world.

Nor was it ever a problem getting Basil back into the boat once I was ready to go home. Frequently, I'd take him out into the open bay and toss him into the sea to frolic on his own. Always he kept a wary eye on me, not straying more than fifty feet or so. I had only to start the motor and he'd make a dash for the boat. He was fearful of being left alone in that vast unknown.

The relationship was all that I had dreamed of and more. I saw it as the beginning of a long and rewarding friendship. It didn't turn out that way. The final chapter in Basil's short life is something I find difficult to dwell on. On August 12 that summer, I set out to hunt great white sharks, with Basil along for company. I'd planned to go ashore on one of the uninhabited islands in the course of the day to swim and play with him in the shallows.

Off Mark Island, I was peering ahead to locate the gut between the island and Robinson's Rock. As I adjusted my course, I noticed that Basil's place in the bow was vacant. I wasn't unduly alarmed. He'd been restive, and I figured he'd gone in for a quick dunk.

Then, to my horror, I saw blood on the water. And as I stared at the telltale stain, a dorsal fin cut the surface. A great white shark breeched to feed on the remains of blood and flesh.

In an instant I had a harpoon in hand. With all my aroused strength I plunged the iron into the shark's flank. The water boiled as the wounded sea beast thrashed to free himself from the barb. Then he submerged and I found myself being towed toward the open sea.

I have no clear remembrance of the subsequent battle. I do recall my awe of the terrible power with which I was contending. There was fear, too, or the coppery taste of blood in the mouth, which can be a by-product of fear. I'd battled with great white sharks before, but this struggle was not like any other: This was a direct conflict with my personal nemesis.

Suddenly the line slacked. The shark had surfaced, turned, and was bearing down on my little boat's quarter. The boat shuddered at the impact of the ramming head and underslung teeth. As the shark fell away, as if for another charge, the boat rose in the sea and I saw shark's teeth imbedded in the planking.

And that was the end of it. The charge had been a final act of defiance. I had no idea how long it had taken me to subdue the monster; my watch told me it had been something over two hours. Spent, I looked down at the primitive machine of destruction, now inert and awash. I lit a cigarette, dragged the smoke deep. Then I made the line fast to the stern and bow of my boat and began the long tow back to the harbor.

That morning I'd promised some children I would show them my baby seal. They were there waiting when I tied up. I could only tell them there would be no baby seal to see that day. The shark went twelve feet and weighed 1,200 pounds. I opened up its stomach and there was Basil—in three pieces.

That fall was a lonely time for me. It was only after his death that I realized how much the engaging little rascal had gotten under my skin. I was completely hooked on harbor seals, and over the long winter I came to accept my addiction. Come what may, I would have another. Admittedly, my luck had not been good, but with the true gambler's optimism, I had visions of success in the offing: My third seal would be a winner.

And indeed, there was something propitious about the advent of Andre.

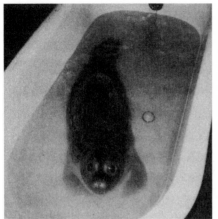

(l) An old bath tub in the basement became Andre's first playment. (Goodridge collection) (r) Like any kid, Andre enjoyed playing the snow. (Goodridge Collection)

Sue and Toni with month–old Basil. (Jim Moore)

Harry with Basil. (Sari Bunker)

5

Andre's First Summer

The summer of 1961 was the summer of Andre.

Andre's adjustment to his new world was a breeze. Much like a cat's, his curiosity sent him sniffing and peering into every nook in the house. The Goodridge family neither dismayed nor impressed him. He had never before set eyes on a human being, yet he seemed to accept us unquestioningly.

I didn't face him at once with his substitute mother. I wanted him to be hungry, figuring that if he was hungry and seeking sustenance, the connection could be simplified.

That proved to be the case. Late in the afternoon, after he had fully explored the premises, I set the neoprene rig in front of him on the kitchen floor. He looked at it, and then at the assembled family. Intrigued, he bellied over and nuzzled the rubbery surface. As earlier with Basil, I had warmed the target dimple. Andre found it and took to the formula like a bear to honey.

All of us let out our breath in relief. Carol paraphrased the *My Fair Lady* professor's exclamation: "By George, I think he's got it!"

He had indeed. Nor were there any further problems in this department. At least, not for Andre. For me, there was the unwelcome chore of turning out of a warm bed in the night to prepare the formula. Thalice took a sort of perverse delight in my tours of duty. She had been through it with five kids, getting up in the middle of the night while I lay abed. I must say, she had the good grace not to gloat out loud.

Although I made a place for Andre in the cellar, he had the run of the house and yard during the day, and at least twice a day we went down to the sea to swim. It was during these swimming sessions that I observed something about a young seal that was curious, at least to me. Andre did not like to get wet! I'd toss him in the water, and almost at once he was out again. Even when I went in with him in my scuba gear, out he would plop. I decided it was useless to try that kid's challenge, "Last one in is a rotten egg!" It would have done no good. Andre simply preferred the warm sun.

I recalled that my earlier seal pups had had the same distaste for chill Maine water, so clearly Andre wasn't just being difficult. Then I remembered something else, which confirmed a dawning suspicion that this reluctance was normal seal-pup behavior. Seal pups do not have a thick layer of fat for insulation; also, lacking this blubber, they are less buoyant.

Thinking back, I recalled the amusing sight of a seal mother on the ledges trying to coax her young into the sea. Commonly, she would splash water into a sleepy pup's eyes with a flipper, much as a human mother splashes her toddler at the beach. But the seal mother doesn't necessarily let it go at that. If the pup refuses to respond to its mother's blandishments, the mother very likely will push her offspring into the water.

Seeing a mature harbor seal's perfect adaptation to the sea, it's difficult to accept that a seal pup, though it may not have to learn to swim, seems to lack complete confidence in his ability to stay afloat.

The young pup will cling to the mother and frequently ride above water on her head.

I'd observed mother otters in the wild cope with the same kind of timidity. A mother otter will carry the pup on her head into deep water, then suddenly submerge, leaving the surprised youngster to sink or swim. Left to its own devices, the pup quickly learns its aquatic capability.

Again, I faced the problem of weaning. My earlier experiences with "motherhood" simplified matters. After two weeks, I began emulsifying fish and adding it to the formula. In three weeks I used heroic treatment and force-fed him herring and mackerel.

Once Andre was on fish, life was simpler for all concerned, but I realized that my responsibilities were not over. Lacking a natural mother, would the pup get the hang of catching his own food in the sea? Aquarium seals never have to forage for themselves; they become dependent upon man. I didn't want that to happen to Andre. Since there was little I could do to teach him the art of capturing food, I could only let him go off on his own and hope for the best.

Each day I'd release him at the harbor and leave him. If he departed for good, that was fine with me. Originally, my intention had been to enjoy his company for a few summer months. In my mind there had never been the question of *whether* he would return to the wild, but *when*. I wanted him prepared.

Each night I would go down to the waterfront. He would be there waiting to be fed and picked up. His favorite rendezvous was under the town float. I'd pick up a deck board and there he would be.

Then one day, to my delight, he refused the fish I offered him. He appeared to be thriving. I knew then that he had mastered the art of hunting. I assumed that, having achieved self-sufficiency, he would take full advantage of his freedom and depart. He did not. He felt a need for company, and since human company was the only kind he knew, the Goodridge family became the center of his universe. It wasn't a matter of the Goodridges adopting Andre; Andre adopted us and moved right in.

When it was time to go for a swim, he humped right into the backseat of the car and off we'd go. I taught him a few simple tricks, such as rolling over, clapping his flippers, and shaking hands, which he did on command, and sometimes without prompting when he wanted attention or a handout. Soon small audiences began to gather at feeding time. Andre seemed to enjoy doing his tricks for them.

The animals and barnyard fowl adjusted reasonably well to the new recruit. Toot, the fat beagle, was tolerant far beyond the call of duty. I was sitting at my desk late one afternoon when Paula called me from the yard.

"Hey, Andre just kicked Toot out of his doghouse."

There was Toot, dozing on the lawn. Andre was inside the doghouse, curled up on the hay. Toot couldn't be shamed into sticking up for his rights. He was just naturally amenable.

That first summer was a season of social exploration, for both Andre and myself. It was an even exchange. In the beginning, Andre knew as little about people as I knew about harbor seals. Looking back, I can see that I had a slight advantage: I knew·Andre was a harbor seal and belonged offshore among the islands. Andre had no way of knowing that it wasn't exactly normal for a seal to live in a house, associate exclusively with people, and drive to a harbor in the backseat of a car.

The villagers, with a few exceptions, accepted Andre's judgment of his place in the community. All Maine villages have their town characters; very quickly, seal Andre qualified as a member of this select company.

I have lived in Rockport for thirty years. It is a prideful little community. The people are friendly and unassuming. State-of-Mainers have been accused of being cool to newcomers by those who misunderstand the attitude of caution. "You have to summer 'em and you have to winter 'em" is the local way of expressing this wait–and–see attitude. Rockporters know what they have, and if they can't keep it to themselves, they hope at least to minimize the pressures of change.

The village proper is off Route 1. Casual motorists can—and most do—barrel right on through and never know they've been there. This is all right with Rockporters. They prefer not to be noticed. Each spring at town meeting, the local Chamber of Commerce tries to get a respectable appropriation for promotion, but all it manages to wangle is a few hundred dollars.

We have a fine deepwater harbor with a good holding bottom. The cove is well protected, except from a due southerly. In the summer months, the inner harbor is crowded with pleasure craft, which compete for mooring space with the more slovenly fishing boats. Lobstermen, habitual grumblers, mutter about this, mindful at the same time that these summer people keep the price of lobsters right—so right, in fact, that local people can't afford to eat lobsters as often as they would like.

Not too much goes on in Rockport today. It was not always thus. Rockport was a lively commercial port before the century's turn. Scores of wooden sailing vessels—two-, three-, and four-masters—were built on its steep and rocky shores. And from wharves long since rotted away, ice was shipped down the coast and as far as the West Indies. Lime was the big industry in the last century. The remains of kilns for the burning of lime rock still may be seen among the rank weeds along the shore. A few old-timers are still alive who can recall the days when a man could walk across the cove on "wood-ers," vessels that brought in cordwood to fire the kilns.

I am involved in town affairs to a limited degree. I hold the post of tree warden, and for a number of years I've acted as harbor-master. The job doesn't pay anything, but the town fathers figure that so long as I'm out in my boat every day anyway, I might just as well look out for things in the harbor.

It's the waterfront I know best, of course. What action there is in the village is there; at least, all the action that matters to me. A half-dozen lobstermen and one draggerman base in the cove. Of the lobstermen, only Howard Kimball is what could be called a full-timer. Also, he's the only fisherman who has a wharf on the shore. Howard lobsters from spring until December and crabs in the win-ter months. His wife, Gladys, picks out the crabmeat and makes a good thing of it. Howard also stops off the cove when the herring strike into the harbor, which is maybe once or twice a summer.

And then there's Al Eaton. Al's getting along now and he's mellowed some, but there was a time when his bucko-mate voice could be heard all the way out to Indian Island. Al is the eyes and ears of the waterfront. If you want to know what boats are in or out, or the state of the tide, or what weather the sky promises, you ask Al.

The cove fishermen looked out for Andre that first summer. Actually, they had no feelings about seals one way or the other. They saw seals on their rounds and took them for granted, as they did the gulls and shags. Many of them would shoot seals that got into a fish weir or tore up the fishermen's nets, but, by and large, harbor seals were something they could take or leave alone.

Andre was different. Andre was one of their own. Mainers are inclined to indulge their local characters, human or otherwise. Back a way, there was a black mutt named Peppy. Peppy wouldn't hunt unless he first had an ice-cream cone. Anyone could take him hunting and he'd wait in front of the corner store for a bird hunter to come along. The price of his services was a treat of an ice-cream cone. No ice-cream cone, no hunting. And we had a boxer who slept in the middle of the street in front of the post office. No one thought to ask him to move; you simply drove around him.

Andre liked to have his belly rubbed. He'd swim alongside a rowboat and roll over on his back. Fishermen fell into the habit of rubbing Andre's belly with an oar. And though they were not exactly overjoyed when he took to sleeping around in their boats or on top of their gear, they soon got accustomed to his loose behavior.

Andre developed another habit as the summer progressed—one that was not so easy to cope with. Like a kid who begins feeling his oats, Andre began wandering off to explore the world around him. He'd gone overnight, and then for a day or two at a time.

So I worried. Strangers who didn't know that Andre thought he was people would expect him to act like a seal. Goodness knows how some lady down the coast would react at finding a seal asleep on her back porch. And I thought about the possibility of some zoo hunter's coming upon this friendly harbor seal and selling him to an aquarium. My point was simply that if he wasn't going wild, I wanted him as a member of my family, and not exploited in some commercial enterprise.

When he didn't show up on the evening of the Fourth of July, I set off down the coast to look for him. While I was off, Thalice got a call. He was down on the Camden wharf, some miles to the east, having the time of his life. He was showing off his few tricks before a crowd of amused spectators. Thalice drove to Camden and picked him up.

Andre was developing with amazing speed. He'd more than

doubled his weight in only three months. I could still manage handily to carry him to my car each night, but how much longer this would be possible, I wasn't at all sure. I thought about that mythical farm boy who lifted his calf each day, figuring that by this method of slow progression, he'd have the strength to lift a cow when the time came.

I came to learn that such swift development was typical of a harbor seal. Its puppyhood, the most vulnerable period in a harbor seal's life, is brief. And vulnerable the harbor seal pup must be, because it is estimated that no more than 60 percent survive this short period. The richness of the mother's milk is one factor that makes a two- to three-week lactation period possible, an incredible crash performance in view of the fact that the sea lion's lactation span extends to six months.

Even more astonishing than Andre's physical development was his mental and emotional growth. We humans like to think of a sense of humor as exclusively a talent associated with the higher vertebrates, man in particular. Too easily do we accept the textbook notion that everything an animal does is programmed in its chromosomes, and one way or another directly related to survival. Anyone who has observed animals closely knows this is nonsense. Animals very often do things for fun—just for the hell of it.

A few weeks after Andre's Camden excursion, he was off again, this time for a week. One noon I got a call from a newspaper fellow I knew. He told me Andre was asleep in a boat at Glen Cove, three miles in the opposite direction.

I found him quickly enough, but he wanted to play. I pulled the boat in by its painter. Andre jumped overboard and came up just out of my reach. I went for him and he ducked, bobbing up at a tantalizing distance from me. He had a puckish look in his eye, and I realized at once he was having fun. I couldn't very well explain to a three-month-old seal that I had other—what I considered more important—things to do at that moment.

"Okay," I said, "enough of this nonsense. If you don't want to ride, you *swim* home."

I drove to the Rockport waterfront. In about a half-hour, he arrived. Apparently he realized that the fun was over. He didn't protest when I picked him up and took him home.

Toni was a good match for the little rascal. I'd put an old bathtub in the cellar and filled it with water, a sort of seal playpen. He'd lie low in the water as though sleeping. If someone chanced by, he'd rouse himself suddenly and splash the unwary one with his flippers. One Sunday he soaked Toni when she had her best clothes on.

Toni went down to the waterfront with me the next day. She took a syringe and loaded it with water. When Andre poked his head over the side of the float, she let him have it in the face. He ducked and came up again in another spot. She squirted him again. This went on for quite a time, and I was about to tell Toni to lay off when I realized Andre was enjoying the teasing session as much as she was.

One afternoon, in the shallows where Goose River flows into the harbor, Andre was in one of his playful moods. Susan had come with me to pick him up, and it was getting late. Andre decided to play hide-and-seek. Each time we went to grab him he'd hide behind some floating seaweed. He'd wait until our search got warm, and then off he'd dash to secrete himself again.

Susan had waded out up to her knees. Suddenly she pointed back toward the shore. "There's that little brat. He thinks he's hiding."

There was Andre behind some seaweed, with only his goggle eyes showing. What he didn't realize was that his whole rump was out of water. He was a surprised pup when Sue simply walked over and picked him up.

The summer went quickly, as summers do. In Maine, summer is no more than a brief prelude to autumn. Fall, on the other hand, has a long, slow fuse. It begins in late August with cool nights and clear northwest days. In September the leaves begin turning and the insect hum slowly dies. You can expect light frosts in late September and killing frosts in early October. For two months, Maine people prepare for the winter ahead.

Though we didn't discuss it openly, we were all thinking about Andre's future as November came and ice began forming at the edges of the river. What would happen when the harbor froze over, as most surely it would?

The harbor seal is nonmigratory, moving only in his search for food. If inshore fish stocks diminished, as normally they would in the winter months, I could supply Andre with sufficient food to carry him over. The local fishermen had offered to help and, in fact, Howard Kimball early that summer had been giving Andre a cut of the herring he took stop-seining.

I began stockpiling fish in the freezer to meet the contingency. Of course, the big question was: Fish or no fish, would Andre opt to remain? I was concerned and, at the same time, curious. Would he leave in search of food, or were his emotional ties to man and to Rockport Harbor, the only home he had ever known, already fixed and irreversible? In short, had Andre come to the point of no return to the wild? This I would find out soon enough.

By early December, skim ice had begun to form in the inner harbor where the freshwater from the river mixed with the brine of the sea. This was no problem for Andre; he simply shouldered up through it. Nor was he impeded when the ice thickened to two inches and more. He kept a hole open near the wharf, and there he was each afternoon at almost precisely the same time.

Since he still refused the frozen fish I offered, I knew he was still finding food in the sea. And the fact that he didn't come for food was reasonably good evidence that these rendezvous were strictly social. Frequently, Toni or another of the children came with me. He seemed to enjoy that.

In mid-December the floats were taken up. It was no longer possible to get to his ice hole and make physical contact with him. Still he came, bobbing up out of the black hole at the appointed hour. I can only suppose that he was checking up on the family as much as we were checking up on him. He wanted to be sure that he still belonged.

Then came that day in late December that I will never forget. Ice forms in a Maine cove in still, cold weather. When a wind builds up a swell, the ice will break up into jagged floes. That morning I awoke to the sound of a honking northeaster. I dressed quickly and went down to the waterfront.

My worst fears were confirmed. The ice had broken up and the floes were grinding and buckling in the sea surge. Andre's hole was gone. I knew that a young seal's head could be crushed like a grape by that savage ice action.

I didn't say a word to the family about my fears. I went down the next day, and the next. The sea had calmed by then. But there was no sign of Andre.

I broke the news one night before supper.

"Andre's gone," I said.

I realized from the shocked silence in the room that, no matter what I thought, *gone* was the wrong word to use in breaking the news.

I corrected myself at once. "Andre's left," I told the kids. Whatever the truth, it sounded better that way.

6

Andre's First Journey

A Maine winter has a discernible rhythm. December is a friendly month. The fall chores have been done and the last of the summer visitors have departed. Maine people have the state to themselves. It's a sociable time. The ladies put on their church sales and suppers; the men have time to get to know one another again—to talk of the hunting season past and the chances of the Red Sox in the season ahead. All over Maine the lights of Christmas go on.

January is the month of cold, subfreezing days and subzero nights. The old houses creak as the cold penetrates ancient timbers. The January thaw, if it comes at all, is little more than a brief spell of slush and icicles, glittering on rimed eaves.

February is the month of snow, the heart of winter, the time of white stillness. By the time February has run its course, winter for many is like a guest who has outstayed his welcome.

We had enough snow to satisfy anyone that February of 1962. So high were the white barricades thrown up by the highway plows that you could see only the tops of cars as they moved down the road outside our house. We'd put out food for the birds, those that normally wintered here and the foolish ones that decided to try out a Maine winter.

Fifteen or twenty species came to our feeders that February, among them chickadees, evening grosbeaks, redpolls, purple finches, nuthatches, siskins, and jays. Each winter a few old robins remain, aware perhaps that they do not have the strength to make the migration. And, oddly, we had one mockingbird that winter, a bird that is rare in Maine, even in the summer.

By that time, we had all more or less been reconciled to the loss of Andre. For a month or more after his disappearance I'd gone down to the shore each day in the wan hope that he would appear. Now I was convinced that Andre was gone for good.

The loss of Andre meant the end of my seal adventures. I'd vowed not to try to bring up another seal. I began to consider the possibilities of adopting a young dolphin and taking it on as an undersea companion. This would entail a period of training, and with this in mind I built a floating pound. I went so far as to experiment with training by whistle, using good old beagle Toot as a guinea pig.

It was snowing hard that February day when I picked up my mail at the post office and came back up to the house with it. In with the bills was a letter from a neighbor. In the letter was a clipping from the *Marblehead* (Massachusetts) *Messenger* that told of a friendly seal who had become the darling of Marblehead's local fishermen.

The seal was called Josephine. For some weeks she had been loafing and sunning around that North Shore waterfront. I was interested, certainly, but I didn't make any mental connection until I read to the end of the story. Josephine liked an appreciative audience. When she attracted a satisfactory crowd, she'd do a few tricks and beg for a handout.

Now that was familiar! I looked more closely at the photograph that accompanied the story. I let out a roar. There was no mistake! That Marblehead Josephine was Rockport's Andre, 180 miles from home.

Immediately, I got on the phone and called the Marblehead paper. I got the editor, a hard-boiled old guy, judging from his voice. I told him who I was and why I was calling. He didn't seem at all interested in my tale of a lost seal named Andre.

"Thanks for calling," the editor said gruffly, and hung up.

It wasn't until later that I learned of the basis for his lack of enthusiasm. Another character, this one from Long Island, New York, had been bending his ear about a lost sea lion named Candy. The Marblehead citizenry was up in arms at the very thought that their Josie belonged elsewhere. Josie had acquired a loyal fan club, and some of the kids were going around wearing JOSEPHINE SEAL WATCHERS CLUB shoulder patches.

A bit miffed at the editor's dismissal, I phoned my nephew, Jackie Goodridge, who lived a short distance from Marblehead. I asked him if he'd run down when he got a chance and look into the matter. Jackie had known Andre in Rockport. I was sure he'd have little trouble identifying him.

A few days later Jackie called back. Josephine had left Marblehead for points unknown. "She—I mean *he*—hasn't been seen for a week or more," he told me. "But that *had* to be Andre. I talked to a lot of people. There couldn't be another seal that puts on an act for handouts. Now what?"

"I guess we just wait and hope he's on the way home," I said.

So I waited. A week, two weeks went by. In mid-April I got a report that a friendly seal had been sighted around Newburyport, thirty miles north of Marblehead. That was encouraging. I had no idea where Josephine, née Andre, was heading, but at least he was going in the right direction.

It was on May 18, according to my log, that I had a phone call from the neighboring city of Rockland. A newsman I knew said, "Harry, there's a seal down on McLoon's Wharf. Could it be Andre?"

"It's got to be Andre," I said, and I was off.

During my fifteen-minute drive to Rockland, I had a few uneasy thoughts. After six months of freedom, would the wanderer have any interest in coming home? Would he even recognize me? I recognized Andre quickly enough. He'd gained some weight, but the rusty spots below his neck that only I would have noticed clinched the identification.

I approached to within a few yards and spoke to him. All I got was a drowsy look. Still not sure of his state of mind, I called for someone to bring me a lobster crate. When the crate came, I rolled him into it, carried the crate to the truck, and drove home.

The family was waiting expectantly when I lugged the crate into the kitchen. I instructed everyone, including the cat and dogs, to stand back. I dumped Andre on the floor. We all waited.

I need not have worried. Andre looked up at all of us for a few moments; then he flopped over to the open cellar door and glanced down at his old quarters. He began to explore the premises. Satisfied, he looked up at me with a blasé expression that seemed to say, "I see you still have the same old cat."

Then he flopped on the mat and fell sound asleep.

It was much like the occasion of a new baby coming home from the hospital. The kids went around on tiptoe and spoke in whispers so as not to disturb the sleeping youngster. Friends and neighbors phoned. Newspapers were on the line asking for interviews. One newspaperman dropped by for pictures. I realized for the first time that I had a celebrity on my hands. Andre was the headliner, of course; I was just the fellow with the seal.

When Andre awoke from his snooze, I carried him to the scales and weighed him. He went sixty-four pounds. I took this opportunity to examine him closely. I found a few bruises on his body, and one of his flippers had been badly chewed.

This struck me as curious. Adult bull seals go through a period of fighting in late fall, a phenomenon that has no ready explanation, since it comes well after the mating season. Andre was still technically a juvenile, and therefore unlikely to have been involved in this mysterious rite. Nor did it appear to be a shark wound.

I wondered if Andre, because of his "difference" brought about by his association with man, had been forcibly rejected by his own kind. A tragic possibility, but the only explanation that made sense.

Of more immediate seriousness were the sores I found on Andre's belly. They were badly infected and festering. I sat down and phoned a few aquariums in the East. Yes, they knew all about such infections. The pinnipeds and other marine mammals frequently were thus afflicted in the wild state. Not a thing I could do about it. "The seal may eat and even gain weight, but one day you'll find it dead," I was told.

I wasn't satisfied with this glib diagnosis. I called Mac McDonald and told him about the sores and the authoritative prognosis.

Mac snorted. "We'll see about that."

He came right over, examined the sores, and dispatched me to the local hospital for a sterile bottle and some swabs. When I explained to the lab personnel what I wanted them for, they proceeded to give me all sorts of advice, the gist of which I reported to Mac when I returned.

Mac grunted. "Let them take care of people; I'll take care of animals."

After swabbing the sores and putting the swabs into the sterile bottle, he went off to have the pus cultured. A few days later he called and asked me to come to his office. He handed me a bottle of white capsules. "It's a kind of a staph infection," he said. "Give him nine a day until the sores heal."

My great faith in Mac proved justified. Nothing happened for about ten days; then suddenly I could almost see the sores heal. Nor did the problem arise again.

During this period of Andre's recuperation I kept him in the pound I'd built for a dolphin. Since there would be no dolphin to train, I began to play around with the idea of investigating the harbor seal's natural intelligence. Long since, I'd dismissed the "expert" opinion that a harbor seal is untrainable. Now that Andre appeared to have established his permanent residence in Rockport, here was my chance to explore the seal's nature and test its capacity to learn.

The summer before, I'd observed Andre closely in his natural environment as we swam together in the sea. Andre's identification with me was as close underwater as it was on land. He would leave me for moments at a time, but always he would return to check on me, pressing his whiskered face against my faceplate.

He was perfectly content to have me hold him in my arms underwater. The human impulse would be to struggle in panic. And he delighted in having me hang on to his tail for a submarine ride.

The harbor seal's propulsive power comes from the strong sculling action of the hind flippers. The fore flippers are snugged close to the body for streamlined speed or used for planing and stability. The fur seals and sea lions, on the contrary, swim with their fore flippers, while their hind flippers are relatively inactive.

The harbor seal is, of course, an air-breathing mammal, and as dependent upon oxygen as man. Although I didn't wish to test

Andre to his limits, I was curious to know just how long a seal could go without air. Though I did not test Andre to his limits, I did note that fifteen minutes without oxygen caused him little or no stress. Many times that summer I observed him apparently sleeping on the bottom for periods of up to fifteen minutes. The very act of *not* struggling was a conservation measure; underwater struggle results in an excessive use of oxygen.

Oxygen is stored in the blood, and the seal carries one and a half times the amount of blood of like-size land animals. When a seal dives, its metabolism slows down, the heartbeat dropping from 150 beats a minute to roughly 10. Under the water, automatic reflexes shut off the blood flow to all but the most essential organs, further reducing oxygen consumption. The seal's lungs are larger than man's; moreover, the seal can fill its lungs completely in a gulp, hyperventilating in an instant. Submerged, the seal is in a state of neutral buoyancy, and requires little energy to propel its streamlined body through the water. To all this add the fact that the seal has a far greater tolerance for carbon dioxide than man has, and you see the result of at least 20 million years of marine evolution.

The harbor seal, like the other pinnipeds and the whales and dolphin, is a re-entrant. All life began at the edges of the sea. The seals wandered up the rivers and developed on land, only to return to the sea when competition for food became harsh.

I entertained another whimsy that summer. Man has begun to explore the inner space of the planet. Was man in the process of following the seal back to the sea, and for the same reasons? Watching Andre's perfect adaptation to his watery world, I concluded that man has a long way to go before he will be prepared for this adventure.

There was envy mixed with my awe of sealdom. If indeed man is in the process of returning to the sea, that is the way to go. The seal life is the Good Life. Compared to the grim and unrelenting struggle in which terrestrial animals are engaged, the seal lives the life of Riley. Little wonder that the harbor seal is such a genial and easygoing fellow.

One thing I knew as I began to prepare Andre for a training regimen: If I was to succeed, I would have to make it fun. Not even the rewards of fresh fish would make a slave of this free spirit of the sea.

Andre enjoyed napping on various boats in Rockport Harbor. (Goodridge Collection)

7

Andre Becomes a Celebrity

Although this is the story of Andre, a Maine harbor seal, it must unavoidably be told from my point of view. Needless to say, a seal lacks the tool we call language. Andre can tell me when he's hungry, but he has no word for *fish*.

Nonetheless, we have little trouble communicating. Andre holds a slight advantage: He seems to know what's on my mind most of the time, but I'm not always certain what goes on in his. Perhaps this is just as well.

Someone once remarked that it would be interesting to read *Moby Dick* from the whale's point of view. It would indeed. I'd like to listen to what Andre has to say about the present arrangement, if only as a courtesy.

I don't expect I'll ever learn all there is to know about Andre, but certainly my long association with harbor seals has confirmed my youthful conviction that animals are well worth knowing.

Andre's training began during his recuperation from his infection. It wasn't my intention to display Andre. What was to become a tradition of regular evening performances came about by happenstance. I found it necessary to confine him to his floating pound and feed him each day during his convalescence. After my day's work was done and I'd had my supper, I'd bring a ration of fish to the pound. I'd feed him and we'd socialize a bit, going through his routine of tricks. Once these "play–times" became regularized, word got around quickly. Crowds began to gather at the seawall. Soon, Andre's fan club began to expect a show every night, and both Andre and I found ourselves working command performances.

I didn't object to the attention. I must confess there's a bit of the ham in me. Andre seemed to enjoy the applause, too; it gave him a chance to exercise his highly developed sense of play.

I've never thought of such displays as educational. I've been to many of the aquariums where marine animals perform for people more for their amusement than enlightenment. Seeing animals perform gives people a nice comforting feeling of superiority.

"He's almost human!" is the most common response to Andre's repertoire. Man cherishes the delusion that he is the center of the universe. Invariably, he will view what he sees in terms of human behavior. Moreover, he will be inclined to rate animal intelligence according to the degree to which it conforms with human behavior.

I much doubt that it occurs to the fellow in the shorts and funny hat that Andre isn't acting "almost human" when he pushes a ball to me; he's acting like a seal. Seals have been pushing things around with their noses since before man learned to throw his first rock.

A seal requires no training to retrieve. He is a natural retriever. Although wary, he is also naturally inquisitive. Andre will investigate any unusual sound so long as it isn't loud or frightening. He will investigate any strange object as well. It's a myth, of course, that a seal can be charmed by music. A seal has little interest in music as such, but if I should play a guitar, he most certainly would swim over and investigate.

Although few seals have been trained in recent times, there

have been historical instances of harbor seals tamed by man. A century or more ago, a guard on an island in the Firth of Forth had a seal that accompanied him to the mainland in a small boat and guarded the boat while he was ashore. Reputedly, the seal was also trained to catch fish in the sea for his master.

According to a yellowed clipping someone sent me a few years ago, a pair of "learned harbor seals" entertained audiences at the Aquarial Gardens in Boston. The date of the clipping was November, 1859.

My motive for establishing a regimen of training was not to exploit Andre or entertain an audience. I simply wanted to prove to myself that harbor seals are trainable. I'd been rather awed by what trainers had accomplished with animals. I learned to my astonishment that training an animal endowed with the high intelligence of a harbor seal is not nearly as complicated as I had been led to believe.

I didn't consider myself a professional trainer, nor do I today. However, I appear to have a way with animals. My early association with them had taught me one thing of cardinal importance: You don't get very far with wild creatures unless you respect their intelligence. To succeed, the first step is to shuck off any attitude of condescension.

We refer to the man who beats his wife as a "beast," when it should be noted that man is the only animal given to such ungentlemanly behavior. Unthinking, we call the fellow who stuffs himself a hog, when, as a matter of fact, a hog is rather a finicky eater. It's all very well to dismiss a flighty lady as a "birdbrain," but if you think of a bird as stupid, you'll never succeed in getting to know one.

An old fellow in Maine who has been very successful in taming wild birds at his feeder put the rule this way: "Whether you believe it all or not, always try to behave as if a bird can and does reason, as if in some things he is smarter than you."

From the beginning I had an advantage over most professional trainers. I had spent hours with Andre in his world, and I knew him to be a great deal smarter than I in many ways.

I had another advantage. I'd learned as a youngster, and later from my children, how quickly a wild creature will recognize a friend. Children are believers. They accept animals as equals and readily identify with them. When Toni was little she treated wild birds as friends. Because she liked them, she assumed that they liked her.

Not being a professional trainer—that is, my living didn't depend upon the exploitation of an animal's intelligence—I was not obliged to "teach" Andre anything. A bear must be taught to ride a bicycle; a poodle must be taught to walk around on its hind legs and drink tea. Andre has never been asked to do anything he did not do naturally.

A seal will stretch voluptuously and in the process commonly cover his eye with a fore flipper, oddly like a child who is told he should be ashamed of himself. When I caught him in this position one day, I said, "Aren't you ashamed of yourself, Andre!" and gave him a fish. Once he responded to that direction, I worked it into some stage business. He might splash me with a flipper or nip my trouser leg and then, on command, he'd assume that attitude of contrition. It was astonishing to me how quickly he got the idea.

A seal spanks the water with a fore flipper as a warning of danger to a pup, much as a beaver slaps the water with its tail when alarmed. I'd set fire to a piece of newspaper and drop it on the deck of my boat. When it was flaming briskly, I'd tell Andre to put it out. He'd splash until the fire was extinguished. No problem.

I'd watched Andre after he'd been fed and was feeling good. He had a habit of arching his body and nibbling on his hind flippers, often holding this rocker pose for some moments. I caught Andre in this posture one day. I said, "Pose for the camera, Andre." Once he had this command, I used it when I saw a camera in the crowd pointed at him.

Once Andre had a command, he never forgot it. I might forget some piece of business for months, even for a year; Andre never did. It would always be there, stored in his brain when I called for it.

I began by using a whistle to tell him when he was doing something right. Now and again in the beginning he'd get a bit confused. I might ask him to clap and he'd put a flipper over his eyes. When he didn't get a fish, he'd try a few more tricks until the whistle blew and he knew he'd hit it right.

When I began working up some new and more complicated business, the whistle came in handy. Andre's snort is rather a derisive sound. I decided something could be done with that. One evening, I was looking at the dolphin Flipper on television. Andre was there with me. Suddenly I turned to him and asked, "What do you think of the movie star, Flipper, Andre?"

He was quite aware that I was trying something new. He went through his whole repertoire. Finally, possibly in disgust, he snorted, rendering a very good imitation of the ballpark raspberry. I blew the whistle and yelled, "That's it, Andre!" Obviously, Andre didn't appreciate the joke, but he did appreciate the audience reaction when I tried it out the next day at the waterfront.

Sometimes when I'd blow the whistle during these training sessions, I could almost see his mind working. He seemed to be wondering to himself, "Just what was it I did right?" And I could all but see the satisfaction he felt when another run-through clarified the matter.

It wasn't long before I found that the whistle was unnecessary. Nor did I need to rely on hand signals or stresses on key words. I was completely flabbergasted. You train a dog to "sit," "stay," or "heel" with simple one-word commands, accompanied by hand signals. Here I was directing Andre with complicated sentences, spoken in a casual tone of voice.

I had been told by Andre Cowan, for whom Andre was named, that it's very difficult to get the same response from an animal with a number of different commands. Cowan, at the time I met him, was the trainer at Marineland in Florida. We became good friends and corresponded regularly until his death a few years ago. Cowan's point was that you risked confusion and possibly neurosis if you directed a subject in a number of ways to do the same thing.

So convinced was I of Andre's sophistication that I decided to ignore Cowan's observation. Andre's most common vocal expression is the vibrant snort, produced by a sudden expulsion of air through his nostrils, that I worked into the Flipper business. With a little work, I found he would make subtle variations of that raspberry on four or five different commands. There is little difference in the sounds produced by a nose blow, a juicy kiss, and a raspberry, but Andre, upon direction, would produce the correct variation, unerringly.

I tried to explain to a friend what it was about Andre's capacity to differentiate that I found so phenomenal. When he didn't get the point, I said, "I know it must seem complicated to you, but it isn't to Andre."

As I mentioned earlier, I'm not always sure of what goes on in Andre's mind. Obviously, he's motivated by his fondness for fish, but I can't discount the very real possibility that he also enjoys the feeling of accomplishment. That summer I discovered that he definitely responded to applause. This was amply demonstrated as the audiences increased and Andre realized he was the center of attention.

There was one bit of business that he found especially rewarding. I'd hung a motorcycle tire in his pound, stringing it several feet above the water. I thought the toy might amuse him and help to pass the time. Although a seal is not a leaper to be classed with a dolphin, he will breach and "porpoise" in his wild habitat in playful exuberance. A mother seal frequently leaps over her young, apparently in an effort to coax her pup to submerge and follow her.

Andre would arch through the small hoop beautifully and without effort. One day, I discovered him resting in the tire, draped over it like a limp rag doll. I decided to work out a little routine to capitalize on this rather ridiculous posture. Getting him to go through the hoop presented no problem, but the stickler was to direct him to get hung up on command.

So I talked the matter over with him. I've always had the habit of talking to animals as I would to an adult human. They may not understand the palaver, but they do appreciate the personal attention. Andre was to go through the hoop several times as slick as a whistle. Then I would turn to the audience and say, "What you've seen is the result of hours of practice. Now you'll see what he did when he was first learning."

Understandably, I expected to have a problem bringing off that bit of nonsense. Don't ask me how Andre knew when he was expected to leap and get himself hung up in that tire; I used no whistle or special stress on key words. The only change I made for the foul-up part of the business was to move to another part of the platform.

The applause that greeted the first enactment of that routine was the making of Andre as a ham actor. He hung there in the tire and looked up at the crowd. He did everything but bow. Ever since, he has turned his eye to the audience at the conclusion of this performance, accepting the applause as his due.

Another piece of business came about by accident; at least, it was entirely unexpected. While I was working with Andre one summer evening, a small out-of-state boy called out, "Hey, how do you catch a seal?"

Andre had a playful habit of grabbing the end of a rope with his teeth and tugging. I had a coil of rope handy. I tied a knot in the end and when Andre submerged, I tossed it out into the water. Immediately, he latched on to it and began to tug. After a strenuous tug-of-war, I hauled him up onto the platform.

"That, son," I said, "is how we catch seals in Maine. It works better, though, if you get to know the seal first."

A variation on this bit of horseplay occurred to me shortly afterward. I would tie the same sort of knot at the end of a boat painter and allow the wind to carry the boat out from shore. I'd say to Andre, "Hey, some idiot forgot to tie up his dinghy. Go out and bring it in, Andre."

In a flash, he would dive and accomplish the mission. Because Andre towed while submerged, the boat would appear to be moving against the wind and without motive power. It was quite an eerie sight.

Our relationship never took on master-underling overtones. I'd learned with my children that you get a lot farther with cajolery than you do with commands. All this was fun and nonsense. I knew it and Andre knew it. And there were times when friend Andre just didn't feel like horsing around. There was one such occasion in the middle of July that turned out to be embarrassing.

My brother-in-law was vacationing at a lake in Maine some fifty miles from Rockport. He'd seen Andre perform and had been so impressed that he called to say he was driving over with his friends to see this flippered prodigy.

"I told them about Andre, and they think I'm pulling their legs," he said.

My brother-in-law arrived with his friends. They were from Massachusetts, but they might as well have been from Missouri: They wanted to be shown.

What they saw that afternoon was a harbor seal sitting there like a bump on a log. Andre looked at me, then at the audience, and flatly refused to perform. I thought at first that he'd looked up at that ring of unsmiling yahoo faces and thought, "Well, if that's the way you feel about it, to hell with you."

I still like to think that Andre is discriminating and nobody's fool, and there are times when he is just plain contrary. But there was good reason for his indisposition that day, as I was to learn later.

In Maine, harbor seals shed in July. Invariably, Andre sheds the third week in July. During this period, he loses weight, is irritable, and prefers to be left alone.

I learned other things about seals from Andre that summer. A harbor seal is capable of short sprints of fifteen knots. I clocked him from a boat a number of times. However, it was his capability of generating top speed from a passive position in a fraction of a second that astonished me.

This breakaway speed was demonstrated when I would toss a fish out over the water to hovering gulls. Gulls are swift and voracious, but, starting from at my side, Andre more often than not would beat the gulls to the fish. At times, when he was a fraction late, he would come out of the water and take the fish from a gull's beak.

In these competitive dashes, I noted, he'd swim just under the surface and leave a wake, something he seldom did in ordinary cruising. I can only surmise that this disturbance was designed to alarm the gull. Andre had nothing against gulls personally. Gulls often gathered around when he was sunning himself, and he ignored them.

I've read that seals sometimes prey on sea ducks, taking them from below when they are rafted. Andre will not bother a duck. One day when, as an experiment, I directed him to retrieve a swimming duck, something he was quite capable of doing, he simply refused.

A seal, when it rests in the water with only its head exposed, "stands" vertically. From this position and in this state of neutral buoyancy, he will either submerge slowly like a submarine or, if startled, use his powerful hind flippers to breach in an arc and dive quickly.

I found that a harbor seal is as much at ease in fresh water as in salt. I would take Andre out to a nearby lake and swim with him for hours. There exists a large colony of harbor seals in freshwater Seal and Harrison lakes in northern Quebec, which were cut off from the salt water of Hudson Bay in the course of the past eight thousand years.

Far more eye-opening than its physical skills was the day-by-day revelation of the harbor seal's extraordinary intelligence. I realized that I was in the company of a most remarkable animal—one that could reason, evaluate, and store knowledge. Not only did Andre have a sense of play; he also possessed a sense of the ridiculous. I was quite aware of his capacity for affection and his uncanny sensitivity to nuances. One memorable day in September I realized that I had fallen far short of a true estimation of Andre's mental and emotional capacity.

My daughter Toni had come down to the waterfront with me one afternoon, wearing a new coat decorated with brass buttons. She reached down to pat Andre's head. Feeling playful, or perhaps puckish, he arched up, nipped one of the buttons from her coat, and dropped it into twenty feet of water.

Toni was distressed, of course. I was quite angry and gave him a real dressing-down. Then I forgot about it.

The next day I went down to the waterfront. Andre was waiting. He dropped the button at my feet.

Andre was as much a member of the family as any pet could be. (Goodridge Collection)

Andre performs his range of tricks, always with a tasty fish for a reward.
(upper and lower left, Lew Dietz; top, Bob Williston; above, Jim Moore)

8

The Long, Hard Winter

As fall came on I once again had a decision to make: I could release Andre and offer him another opportunity to readapt to the wild and his own kind, or I could try to keep him over the winter. He had adjusted well to his floating pound, but the enclosure would not stand up under the action of the harbor ice; nor was there any way to get out to feed Andre once the harbor was icebound.

It was all very well to tell myself that a wild creature's place is in the wild. But was Andre, after this period of association with man, technically wild? It wasn't so much a question of what *I* thought: What did Andre think? After that experience with Toni's button, I had the rather uneasy feeling that Andre was forgetting he was a seal.

The question of what to do was resolved, at least temporarily, when Luke Allen offered me the use of his boat-storage shed on the waterfront. Luke and his wife Norma had been involved with Andre from the beginning. They had come to Rockport about the same time as Andre, and had taken over what once had been a sail loft and was at the time serving as a lobster plant. Norma had established a fine restaurant on the middle floor. Luke used the lower floor and the shed, which housed the lobster holding tanks, for boat storage and repair, which along with a marine facility became his end of the enterprise. The Allens live on the top floor of the building with their four children.

Not only did they enjoy Andre; they were delighted that the restaurant clientele soon came to think of him as a part of the Sail Loft's salty charm. A pump in the shed supplied salt water to the tank where the restaurant's live lobsters were held. This meant that I was assured of a change of water each day. I contracted to have built an eight-by-eight-by-four-foot wooden tank. When the tank arrived, I had it set up next to a window so that Andre might at least have a room with a view.

Andre moved into his winter quarters in early November. My plan was to feed him twice a day and spend some time with him mornings and evenings. Even though he was, at eighty-some pounds, only marginally portable, I decided to carry him to the house every other night or so, to assure him that he was still a part of the family.

Things worked out fairly well that first month. Because the shed was unheated, I was concerned at first about ice forming on the surface of the tank. It was soon apparent that Andre's activity would keep the water from freezing over.

I wasn't at all concerned about the near-freezing temperature of the water. Harbor seals are perfectly adapted to the climate in this northern habitat. The insulating property of a thick layer of fat under the skin prevents excessive heat loss, and what loss occurs is compensated for by a fast metabolism.

The seal's thin flippers would be vulnerable to freezing were it not for the arrangement of the blood vessels. This network is arranged in such a way that the warm blood flowing into the flipper passes very close to the outgoing flow of blood. The mean temperature of the flipper and its blood is maintained at a lower level than in the rest of its body: Heat is not wasted in an effort to keep the flipper warm, but enough warmth is provided to prevent it from freezing.

Nor does the seal attempt to keep the surface of its body skin warm. Although the skin is well supplied with small blood vessels, these can be shut off from the main circulatory system when conditions dictate. In frigid water, only enough blood is permitted through for nourishment and to keep the skin from freezing. A massive temperature gradient of a few degrees above freezing at the surface of its body to a cozy 70 degrees or more inside the blubber layer minimizes heat loss in chilly water that would bring quick death to a human being.

After exertion or basking, the seal is capable of a quick release of excess heat. The blood vessels in the skin are dilated, causing rapid heat loss from the body surface.

I observed this adjustment process when I brought Andre home for the night. He would shiver in the warmth of the kitchen for several minutes before a comfortable adjustment was made. He suffered no ill effects from this sudden change of temperature.

It was during this period that Andre became housebroken. It had never occurred to me to attempt to "civilize" him to this degree. Andre decided on his own to accommodate to the Goodridge menage. Without realizing it, I contributed to his decision. After he would wet the floor, I would go for the mop. Andre disliked the mop slatting around him and would snort at it. Realizing that he associated the mop with his wetting, I took to slatting it around more strenuously. He got the point. I never needed to bring out the mop again.

As the winter progressed I began getting signals that Andre wasn't happy in his confinement. I was distressed too. The sight of him lying there on his platform for hours looking out to sea was heartbreaking. I felt it was risky to release him in the depth of winter with no time to adjust to its rigors. The alternative was to hang on until spring and hope for the best. After all, I reasoned, Maine people get a bit kinky and irritable along about mid-February, and *they* manage to make it through until spring.

Andre demonstrated his increasing irascibility on a number of occasions. A state trooper I knew expressed an interest in seeing Andre. One day he came with me into the shed. He was dressed in a crisp new uniform. Andre took one look at the trooper and with obvious malice slapped a flipper on the water and doused him from head to foot.

The trooper still swears I'd put Andre up to it. I made a point after that of slowing down to posted speed when I saw him on the highway.

On another occasion, Mary Cramer, an ardent local fan of Andre's, brought him a present of four pounds of fresh smelt. She asked me if she could feed him. "Why not?" I said. Andre looked at the fish and then at Mary. His thanks were a loud and juicy raspberry. He plopped into the water and disappeared from view.

"I guess he doesn't like smelt" was all I could think of to say to Mary. The Goodridges had smelt for supper that night.

More and more troubled by Andre's emotional state, I increased the frequency of my visits to the shed. I would try to relieve his boredom by having him go through his bag of tricks. He would perform, but I could see that his actions were perfunctory, that he was only making an effort to please me. His dependence upon my company grew. One day, another door to my understanding was opened. I became aware that Andre "sensed" my arrivals before I appeared.

So far as I had been able to ascertain, very little study has been done on the sense organs of harbor seals. A source book might say, "The harbor seal is reputed to have a good sense of smell." That would be it. Matter of fact, the harbor seal has an incredibly keen sense of smell. This I learned one day in late February.

A seal doesn't breathe as we humans do, in rhythmic inspirations and expirations. A seal's nostrils close after a breath and remain closed until more oxygen is required. Hauled out and resting, Andre would go fifteen minutes or more without taking air into his lungs. Because its nostrils are sealed for protracted periods when resting, a seal relies on its ears for warning of danger. But when it does open its nostrils for air, its olfactory sense is both keen and discriminating.

I slipped quietly into the dark shed that afternoon. A small light burning over Andre's pen enabled me to see him, but he couldn't see me. He was sleeping soundly. I waited in the blackness near the door. Presently, he opened his nostrils for air. In that same instant, he knew I was there. He began slithering about in excitement and craning his neck.

Perhaps even more astonishing to me were the demonstrations of Andre's sophisticated auditory endowment. Perhaps I shouldn't have been astonished. We tend to wonder about things we cannot explain. The six dogs I've had over the years all recognized the particular sound of my car when I would drive up. Andre, however, could identify me when I was in any of five vehicles. I use three trucks in my business, and we have two cars in the family. No matter which I used, he would be alerted to my arrival. I'd noted this acuity the summer before. Andre's pound was moored a good stone's throw from the shore. I'd arrive and park. Before I could step out into the open, Andre would be out of the water and craning his neck, even though there were many other cars coming and going.

*   *   *

It's all downhill to spring is a phrase one hears after the middle of February. This expression of optimism helps Maine people to keep their spirits up. The calendar may suggest that the worst of the winter is over, but no one is fool enough to count on it. Maine people have learned that promises are not to be trusted, and that only when the ice is gone from the back ponds and the peepers begin their vernal choruses in the bogs is spring around the corner.

Rain and fogs had taken most of the snow. All that remained of winter were the grimy hillocks of snow along the highways. Then that sneak northeaster struck. It began in the afternoon, a blinding snow driven by a perilous wind. Knowing there was a good chance that I'd be snowbound the next morning, I brought Andre up to the house for the night. I put him in the cellar and went to bed.

I looked out upon a white world the next morning. It was still snowing lightly, but the storm's fury had been spent. I went down into the cellar to feed Andre. No Andre. I felt a draft and saw a small heap of snow on the cellar floor. Andre had pushed out a pane of glass and departed.

I rushed upstairs and quickly hauled on my boots and parka. I had little trouble following his trail. A trough in the new snow marked his escape route to the water. And there the trail ended.

I looked out beyond the ice floes to the open bay. I could hear the blatting of the foghorn off the Rockland breakwater.

There was no sign of Andre, of course. There was nothing I could do. "Good luck, Andre," I said, and broke trail homeward through the snow.

Over a cup of coffee, it struck me that there was one thing I could do. I called the newspapers. Already in his young life Andre was news. I wanted word out that a friendly seal who thought he was people was on the loose.

It was well that I broadcast the news. A day or so later, I had a phone call from the harbormaster at Round Pond, a small coastal village fifty miles west of Rockport. A seal he presumed to be Andre was there, performing for a group of delighted children.

By the time I got to Round Pond, Andre had vanished. "Y'know," the harbormaster told me, "that seal had a close call. I was in the store when this fellow saw the young seal and went for his rifle. He's a lobsterman, and he has this idea that seals eat lobsters. 'Billy,' I said to him, 'don't it strike you a mite odd to see a seal playing with kids? Could be it's that seal I read about in the paper.'"

I thanked him and asked him to call me if Andre showed up again. And show up he did the next day for another performance.

This time he waited for me. He made no fuss when I picked him up and carried him to the car. On the drive home he fell off to sleep.

*No boat was safe from Andre's explorations. (*Camden Herald*)*

9

Elray

Putting Andre's pound overboard was a festive occasion. Luke Allen used his Travel-Lift to set the floating enclosure in the water. We towed it out to the mooring with his service boat.

After the long winter, anything that happens on those first fine days of spring is bound to be joyous. The gulls cry and swoop, the town dogs romp, and the old men emerge from their winter's durance to sit on the benches in the sun and pick up their remembrances where they'd left off in the autumn.

Spring is a busy time on the waterfront. Hauled-up boats are scraped and painted. Floats are checked and caulked, preparatory to setting over. Tiered lobster traps line the river wall, ready to be put over for spring fishing. A few youngsters, unflagging optimists, fish off the seawall. It's a month before the flounder will show up, and a good three before the mackerel will start running, but what's wrong with not catching fish when the sun is warming and the wind is southerly?

And the most joyous of all was Andre. He swam willingly, even gratefully, into his pen, frolicking like a colt in spring pasture. Aware of the crowd that had stopped work to watch the launching, Andre acknowledged the attention with a few gratuitous leaps.

And again I was struck by Andre's need for people. The nature of my dilemma emerged with a new clarity. Andre was a product of two worlds: His blood responded to the call of the open bay; his heart belonged to the adoptive realm of humankind. The floating pen was not the final answer to the problem. And since he continued to seek out people, as he had at Round Pond and on all his excursions, complete freedom was not the answer either.

The danger lay in his innocence. He did not know how close he had come to sudden death from a rifle bullet. When and how would he learn that, as there were sharks in the sea, there were predators on the land, strangers unprepared for a seal who sought human company.

Not knowing what course to take, I played it by ear that summer. Luke Allen's boy, Ben, joined me that season. Ben was twelve, tall for his age and not yet at ease with his extremities. Luke thought it would be good for the boy to work with Andre, and I thought it would be good for Andre to have a boy for company. Ben fell overboard a few times, but he was an intelligent and willing lad, and soon learned to be useful. He made some spending money when the crowds gathered in the summer by passing a bucket around for Andre's "fish money." He almost fell overboard again when he found a wadded twenty-dollar bill in the bucket one summer day.

Fall rolled around, and I was still weighing Andre's future. Finally, I decided to give the winter quarters in Luke's boat shed another try. I wasn't optimistic. It was well that I wasn't. Andre was in his winter tank for less than a month when I knew that confinement was not the answer. When he languished and refused to eat, I saw that I had no alternative: He would have to be released to take his chances in the winter sea.

Again, I alerted the newspapers. They were there at the

appointed hour in early December, along with a delegation of towns-people. I simply lifted Andre from his tank, set him on the floor of the shed, and said, "You're on your own, Andre. Get going."

He didn't hesitate. He went humping down to the shore on a beeline and belly-whopped into the sea, where he went porpoising around the harbor in great arching leaps. It was a stirring demonstration of pure joy.

He turned back only once. Thalice was there with two of the children. He came toward us just under the surface, breached with a great leap, and spanked the water. Then, with one last slap of his hind flippers, he embraced the sea and was gone.

I had reservations about this valedictory. Perhaps he was gone for good. Then again, perhaps he would enjoy a hobo life for a few carefree days and come home. Goodness knows, he deserved a spree.

I worried about him, of course, and I was relieved when I had a phone call from Rockland. Andre was there in the harbor. I drove over and found him. Although the cove was frozen over, he'd found a bight of ice-free water and was playing in the shallows.

I spoke to him. He spoke right back—with a snort. The animals of Disney's world solve the communication problem by speaking passable English. Andre speaks only his native tongue. But I had no trouble understanding Andre's snort.

What he said was, "Buzz off! I'm not ready to come home yet."

So I buzzed off. I went home to await further reports of his adventures.

Two days later, there was a call from Friendship, a coastal village for which the famed Friendship sloop was named. Andre had reported in there briefly and had departed.

I told myself that Andre was gunkholing, and I would have to wait for more reports on his peregrinations. The Maine term *gunkholing* means cruising casually from one small cove to another as the spirit moves. I hoped Andre's wayward spirit would turn him homeward once the novelty of freedom palled.

A week passed. No calls. When a full month had elapsed without a word, I became uneasy, then seriously concerned. I called the Coast Guard, and I must say I felt a bit silly inquiring of a gruff Coast Guard commander if he had seen any friendly seals lately. It turned out he knew all about Andre, and was quite sympathetic. He promised to alert his forces to the emergency. Since that day I am satisfied that the Coast Guard motto, "Always Ready," is for real.

Then, one day in March, Luke Allen phoned me. "Hey, Harry," he said, "Andre's back in the harbor."

Andre recognized the sound of my car as I drove up to the seawall. He was below on the rocks, craning his neck for a view of me. I was appalled at what I saw. He was lank as a mink and his coat was poor.

"Hey, boy," I yelled, "stand by."

I rushed back to the house, thawed out some frozen fish, and dashed back again. He hadn't moved. He was happy to see me, and even happier to see the fish.

Had poor fishing or homesickness brought him home? Or a bit of each? What I knew for certain now was that Andre was no longer a creature of the lonely outer ledges. If home was, as Robert Frost had put it, "a place where if you knock at the door they have to let you in," Rockport was home to Andre.

This marked the beginning of what I've come to think of as Andre's Town Bum Period. It marked a new period for me as well. Since clearly Andre had made his free decision, I had no choice but to accept the situation. Ours was no longer a passing friendship.

Andre was for keeps. Like it or not, from then on he would be my personal responsibility.

Matter of fact, I was delighted. It appeared that finally we had arrived at an ideal solution. Andre would have his freedom and I would have Andre. He could forage for himself or come to be fed, as he wished. I was satisfied that he wouldn't again wander too far afield.

The more I thought about it, the more nearly perfect the arrangement seemed. He would be good company in the water when I dived for scallops in the fall. It wouldn't even be necessary to whistle him up as a hunter does his dog. I would need only to go overboard and Andre would be there.

And things did work out admirably that fall and winter, for me at least. But by the next spring it was brought to my attention that all was not well. And by the end of that summer, it became quite clear that a seal, who lived on the town and assumed all the prerogatives of a citizen, and additionally some of the privileges of royalty, would present some social complications.

At four years of age Andre wasn't exactly an elder; neither was he any longer a cute little pup. The frisky little rascal who would roll on his back so a fisherman could scratch his belly with an oar was now a mature 150-pound adult who was inclined to view such attentions as his right. He took to nipping at oars, making himself a nuisance.

I was down at the waterfront the morning Dave Grant, a part-time lobsterman, started to push out with his dory to tend his string of traps. Andre appeared and began to plague him. Dave was plying heavy sweeps and pushing against the wind and tide. It wasn't any help at all to have a playful seal grabbing at his oars. Dave got as far as Kimball's wharf and gave up. He came back and yelled to me, saying something about that "jeezley" seal of mine.

I realized that Andre had to be cured. I got into the dory and began pushing out. When Andre grabbed one of the oars, I thumped him with it. He came at it again and I thumped him once more. It required a half-dozen thumps before he was convinced that I wasn't playing with him. He backed off some distance and glared at me.

Dave was able to set out to tend his traps without interference—for that day, anyway.

Then another problem developed, perhaps not so serious, but considerably more difficult to solve. Andre began to take his siestas in moored rowboats and dinghies, half swamping the little crafts in the process of getting in and out. Nor was he gracious about being disturbed. Visiting yachtsmen were particularly hard to placate. They didn't find anything amusing about a seal assuming proprietary rights to their dinghies.

I was hopeful that this problem would be solved in the fall, when most of the boats were hauled up for the winter. It was, in a way. Andre, finding no boats to nap in, took up winter quarters at Howard Kimball's wharf. Kimball's lobster dock is situated halfway out the west side of the harbor. Howard is a genial fellow, endowed with that easy Maine tolerance for offbeat behavior. He liked Andre well enough, and the idea of a vagrant seal in the harbor didn't bother him unduly. But a seal in lordly possession of his gear when he had need of it was something else again.

"Just slat him with an oar when he's a nuisance," I told Howard when he brought the matter to my attention. "He has to learn the facts of life somehow."

"I hate to baste him, Harry," Howard said. "He's sort of a friend of mine."

"If he's not cured, someone who's not a friend might shoot him. Neither one of us would like that."

"I'll baste him a little," Howard said, "and see what happens."

What happened was that Andre stayed out of Howard's skiff but took to basking on the twine and gear on his crowded wharf. If Howard wasn't entirely happy about that, he soon concluded that this was a situation he was going to have to live with. Not only had Andre discovered a sanctuary, he had discovered Elray.

Elray was Howard's boy. Andre fell in love with Elray. And it was clear from the onset of this passion that no amount of slatting with an oar was going to break that affiliation.

Elray was twelve the fall Andre came into his life. Now a fresh graduate of the Maine Maritime Academy with a third mate's ticket in his seabag, Elray recalls his boyhood friendship with a lonesome seal:

"Andre was always waiting when I got home from school. He wanted to play, but I had chores to do. My father took up his lobster traps and went crabbing in the late fall and winter. He'd store the crabs underwater in a crate attached to a pulley line. My job was to get the crabs out of the crate and take them up to the house for my mother to boil and pick for the market.

"I'd haul the crate in and try and set it up on the shore rocks. But there would be Andre. When I'd grab one becket, he'd take aholt of the other becket and commence pulling against me. Now that crate was heavy enough for me as it was, and it sure was aggravatin'.

"But I could tell that he was lonely and wanted company. So I'd talk to him and mess around with him some. I guess he first started coming to our wharf when everything was hauled up at the foot of the harbor. This was the only place there was any action. And maybe kids plagued him a little down at the landing. They'd throw rocks at him. Not cruel or anything, but kids like to have something to throw rocks at, I guess.

"Anyway, like I said, I'd play with him when I had the time. But there were times when I was busy getting crabs for my mother or cleaning up the lobster boat after my father got in from fishing. Andre, he'd keep trying to get my attention. He'd splash water on me with his flipper and nip at my pant leg, or do a few crazy tricks. When I didn't stop my work, he'd get wicked aggravated.

"I can see him now. He'd dive and come up with a mouthful of seaweed and slat it around. You know, like some brat kid. He'd snort and he'd fuss until I did pay attention to him. So I'd stop work and play with him. I'd get a stick and stand on the float and get him to jump for it. I'd keep holding it higher and higher. He'd jump like a dolphin. When he had to make a big jump, he'd go to the bottom and push off with his tail and come clean out of the water.

"Then I'd tease him with a line like you do with a kitten. I'd toss the line in the water and he'd try to latch on to it. I'd yank it before he could grab it. He didn't like it when I was quicker than he was. He'd dive and come up with some weed and thrash and bash it around. So I'd let him grab the line and pat him some and he'd be happy again.

"He could be a real nuisance, of course. I might need the skiff to get out to the mooring to clean up Howard's boat. He'd be in the skiff and he wouldn't want to get out. Howard told me to thump him with an oar. I didn't like to do that, but sometimes I had to. But it seemed the more I'd thump him, the better he liked it. Then he took to nipping at the oar when I'd push out to the lobster boat. Sometimes he'd take an oar right out of my hands.

"But, all in all, it was fun. I didn't have too many kids to play with myself. I knew how lonesome he was. I'd be playing with him and then it would be time to go to eat. He'd be swimming around, and I'd say, 'See you tomorrow, Andre.' He'd follow me as far as the rocks and watch me to the house. He'd look so sorry-eyed. I'd go into the house and look out, and there he would be, still looking.

"It was a great day for Andre when I took up scuba diving. I'll never forget my first encounter with him in the water. It was before I'd got my scuba gear and I was snorkeling. I had no idea he was around. Suddenly he appeared from nowhere. He grabbed me from the rear and put his flippers around me and hugged me. Now that's a real funny feeling, let me tell you, to be swimming in the sea and have something take you from behind like that!

"Later, I got used to him being around when I was diving. In November, when the scallop season opened, I would go scalloping. I would rig up an inflated inner tube with a net to hold the scallops that I would bring up from the bottom. Of course, Andre would want me to play with him, and he could be some aggravatin'. I'd see a scallop on the bottom and go to pick it up and Andre would put his mouth over it and not let me pick it up. It was like he was saying, 'Hey, this is my territory. Leave that stuff be.'

"I soon learned that the only way I could get any scalloping done was to put my arms around him and scratch him under his flippers. He sure loved that. But I never could go diving without Andre. I'd go into the water and there he would be. What he usually did first was push his face against my faceplate. I guess he never could figure out what I was doing behind that glass.

"He had one trick that sure gave me a scare at first. He'd back off just out of sight in the murky water. Then, suddenly, he'd come right at me as though he was going to hit me amidships. At the last moment he'd slip between my legs. When he first did that I surfaced fast by pushing down on his back as he went under me. He thought that was great fun. So after that we'd have to play leapfrog for a spell.

"We had some great times together, Andre and I. Once in a

while in the late fall he'd go off and not appear for a few days. I worried about him. Then he would show up all bloodied. I guess he went to sea to find some seals to play with. But I can only suppose that it didn't work out too well. Or maybe he was looking for a mate and he'd run into some competition. Anyway, he'd come back and we'd be friends again. He'd go diving with me and we'd mess around. I always felt more at ease with him in the water than I did on land. In the water I could take him right in my arms and pat him. I couldn't do that out of water. He came ashore to rest and didn't want to be bothered. The water was the place to play.

"And like I said, he was like a brat kid and would do anything to get attention. He was a real showoff. I remember the day my father got a new movie camera. He brought it down to the shore. 'Hey, Andre,' he said, 'see what I got—a movie camera. Now get out there and do your stuff.'

"Now, you wouldn't believe this, but I swear it's the truth. He put on a show like I'd never seen before. He boiled through the water and went leaping into the air. He dived and brought up seaweed and slatted it around the rocks. He rolled over on his back and splashed with his flippers, all the time with one eye on that camera. Now, how do you explain that? All my father said that day was 'Do your stuff, Andre.' I still haven't figured that one out.

"I guess it was a sad day for poor Andre when the time came for me to go away to school. He still comes to the wharf looking for me to play with him. There's one thing he never did learn: People can't live the way seals do. They can't swim out and get themselves a fish to eat, then lay around on the rocks in the sun until they get hungry again. Andre never could seem to get it into his head that people have to work for a living."

l-r: Elray with his lobsterman father, Howard Kimball, and Harry at the Kimball wharf. This was Andre's favorite winter hangout, and Elray was a friend in need. (Lew Dietz)

Andre's floating pen in Rockport Harbor. (Goodridge Collection)

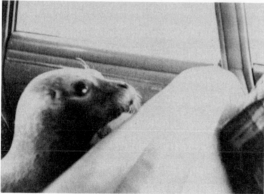

For the first few years of his life, Andre was easily portable by car. He considered it quite normal for a seal to live in a house and be driven down to the sea for his daily swim. (Stan Waterman)

10

Trudy

The friendship with Elray extended over a half–dozen winters and well into Andre's annual six-month confinement, an unhappy compromise that was forced upon me by certain civic pressures. Andre had a host of friends, but his penchant for mischief and loose living didn't endear him to a small minority among the citizenry that was of the opinion that our harbor was no place for a sybaritic, nontaxpaying seal.

One such righteous fellow was taking his small boy for a row in the harbor when Andre appeared from nowhere and, leaping out of the water, bussed the child on the cheek. Startled, the boy burst into tears. The indignant father insisted that his child had been "attacked."

Several days later, the local Sea and Shore Fisheries warden approached me on the waterfront. He had had some complaints. He was reasonable enough. He personally had nothing against Andre, but in his official capacity he was forced to take cognizance of such complaints. "We're going to have to do something about that seal, Harry," he said.

What he meant was that *I* would have to do something about the situation. I agreed. I said that I'd confine Andre to his floating pen until November, when all the boats were up and there would be no one around to be kissed.

I explained the situation to Andre as best I could. Basically good-natured, he accepted the restraints that society had put upon his freedom. I'm sure he had come to realize that as all fish do not run the same size, people, too, are various and not all of goodwill.

The first thing I did once the decision was made was to con-tract to have a larger pen built. The new pound, twice the size of the first, was put over in the spring of 1967. Andre went into his new quarters without any fuss. Nor did he display a disposition to play truant on those occasions at feeding time when I gave him a recess in the open harbor.

I waited until all the boats were up in November. "Okay, school's out, Andre," I said, and opened the pen gate.

He made a few passes around the harbor and off he went. He was off on the bum for a few days. Then back he came. I could see he expected to be fed. So I stocked some frozen fish and began his regular feedings at nine in the morning and seven at night.

From the beginning, I had a sneaking suspicion that the sly rascal was getting away with murder. I knew he was quite capable of foraging for himself. On the other hand, I wasn't sure of how plen-tiful fish were in the open bay at that time of year. I had good reason to know that fishermen were finding fish stocks low, since there were times when I'd have to drive ninety miles to Portland to locate her-ring for my freezer. I'd buy four hundred pounds at a clip when I could find fish. At twenty cents a pound, this was no small financial burden.

Nor was it always convenient to go down to the shore at night in all kinds of weather. In the winter it's pitch black at seven at night. Once the harbor was frozen over, I was never sure where Andre would find an opening in the ice.

I solved this problem one bitter January night. When I failed to locate him in the darkness, I yelled out, "Hey, Andre, what do you think of Flipper?"

Out of the black void came a loud and derisive raspberry. Andre got his fish, and I got home before I froze to death.

There were nights when it was too dark to see Andre, even after I'd found his hole in the ice. I'd push a fish into the icy water and the fish would be taken. Once all the fish were gone, I'd say, "That's all, Andre." I'd wait, then probe the water with my hand. He would be gone out to sea under the ice.

And once again I came up hard against a mystery. For a number of years Andre never missed his daily feedings. No matter what the weather, no matter the extent of the ice field, he appeared at the appointed hours. There were times when the harbor was icebound all the way out to Indian Light and beyond, as far as four miles.

How did he make this dark journey?

I'd observed Andre sleeping at the harbor bottom for somewhat more than fifteen minutes. Hauled out, his span between air intakes was seldom more than that. I was aware that the seal tolerates much more carbon dioxide in its blood than do other mammals. Even so, there were many nights when Andre would come in under the ice for distances that reasonably could not be negotiated in half an hour.

For a number of years I pondered that question. One day, a possible explanation occurred to me. Muskrats and otters are able to rebreathe their own air. An icebound otter expels a bubble of air which ascends and lodges under the ice and is there purified. The otter will push the bubble along under the ice with its nose for when, and if, it is needed. Does the harbor seal employ such a backup system for emergency under-ice journeys? I could think of no other explanation for the mystery.

There were to be a host of other unanswered questions in the ensuing years with Andre, but now he was over four years of age, and there was one immediate and more pressing problem to be faced: Andre had become sexually mature. If I were to be consistent in my wish that he should lead as normal a life as possible under the special circumstances, most surely I'd have to concern myself with his sex life.

Obviously, Andre required no briefing in the "facts of life." My burden was to see to it that he was afforded the opportunity for romance during those periods in the spring when Maine seal cows were ready and willing.

However, in Andre's case, it struck me that there might well be an added complication. How would this exile fare in courtship competition with his wild brothers? I'd witnessed harbor seals in their joyous courtship rituals. Also, I'd seen bull seals in combat over the mating privilege. For better or for worse, I decided that Andre should enter the lists and take his chances.

To my knowledge no serious study has been made of the sex life of the harbor seal. I've observed that the male seal is forever ready to mate. The female, because she must carry the biological burden, puts this essential process in proper order. She will accept a mate only during the period of her estrus. Even then, she will not succumb without a period of courtship.

Nature has made some shrewd accommodations to the harbor seal's way of life. Harbor seals do not migrate, but they do disperse in the winter, primarily in search of food, and regroup each spring in the region of their birth, the cows to drop and nurse their pups and then, in what might appear to be unseemly haste, to accept a mate.

The synchronization of these two functions solves the very practical problem of opportunity. The essential business is accomplished within the short span of a few weeks when the colony is together.

Because the seal's gestation period is somewhat less than a full year, another adjustment is necessary if the whelping is to come at approximately the same time each spring. This is effected by the physiological device of delayed implantation. The fertilized ovum begins to develop immediately after copulation, but then becomes dormant when it reaches the blastocyst stage. In most mammals, the embryo becomes implanted at this phase; in seals, the blastocyst remains free in the uterus some weeks or months before implantation occurs and the growth process continues.

Zoologists have observed large regional variations in the timing of the harbor seal's pupping season. On the West Coast of North America, pups tend to be born later going southeast from Alaska to Washington, and earlier going south from Washington to Mexico. On the East Coast, the pupping season appears to be consistently later going north from New England to Baffin Island. No reasons are apparent for these variations, and I can throw no light on the mystery, except to suggest the obvious advantage to the Penobscot Bay seals of being born in mid-May: The period immediately following this date is the time of the greatest fish plenitude in Maine. It's a logical assumption that seal colonies tend to adjust their pupping season to conform to peak fish availability for their young.

Over the years, I'd learned something about the sex life of the harbor seal. In the course of the several springs I learned considerably more. And so did Andre. Presumably, he made his bid in the wild arena. The presumption was based on the evidences of battle he brought home with him. On a number of occasions he returned torn and bloodied and fairly begged for the protective custody of his pound.

Then, in the spring of 1968, he must have met up with the boss bull seal of Penobscot Bay and come off second best. He hauled out on Howard Kimball's float. His flippers were torn, and there were raw wounds on his throat, the scars of which he carries to this day. He remained there recuperating for three days.

It seemed to me that there had to be an easier way to handle this problem. Perhaps I could buy a potential bride. I knew a fellow in Boothbay Harbor who had set himself up in the business of supplying aquariums. So I drove down to that coastal town to investigate the possibility of acquiring a young harbor seal.

Actually, I had two thoughts in mind: I wanted company for Andre, preferably female, and I had an itch to learn what kind of trainer I was. If Andre was an especially smart male, as I guessed he was, I wanted to find out what I could do with a not-so-bright female.

Bob Davis had a half-dozen seal pups in a tank on the property of the Sea and Shore Fisheries Laboratory. "What I want," I told him, "is the dumbest female in the lot."

Bob said, "That shouldn't be hard to decide. The easiest one to net has got to be the dumbest."

That seemed like a reasonable assumption. I took up the net and took some passes at the females in the tank. They eluded me neatly. Then one small, doe-eyed female pup practically swam into the net.

"Yessir, that's my baby," I said. And off the two of us went for home.

The experiment was a spectacular success. In fact, it was a circus. Trudy, as the bride was dubbed, wasn't sexually mature, but for the present Andre had some lively company. Andre made passes at her, of course, embracing her with his flippers. She would nip him, and then the two would chase one another around the enclosure. Andre honored and protected Trudy, but he was an awful tease, plaguing her much as a school boy might pester his kid sister.

In the beginning, Andre managed to steal Trudy's fish at feeding time. Within a month, Trudy was giving as good as she took. More agile, she was soon beating Andre to the food, and I had to make sure that Andre would get his fair share.

Before that summer was over I was forced to conclude that there is no such thing as a stupid harbor seal—and certainly no such thing as a harbor seal lacking a highly developed sense of play. I'd trained Andre to push a ball across the pen and catapult it into a basketball hoop with his nose. Trudy would wait until Andre was set to shoot, then whack the ball away with her hind flipper. Andre would retrieve the ball and try again, only to be frustrated by Trudy's interference.

Andre soon learned to outsmart his little tormentor. He would pretend to ignore the floating ball until Trudy went for her reward of a fish. As soon as Trudy's back was turned, he would dash for the ball and shoot the basket. If a seal could chuckle, he would have chuckled at his one-upmanship.

It was my hope that the two would grow up together and eventually mate. When I released Andre that fall, I put Trudy in his old quarters in Luke's boat shed. There were a few training experiments I wanted to try, and it was too difficult to get Trudy's concentrated attention in Andre's company. She developed fast both physically and mentally over the next months. And the friendship of the two appeared to be of an undying nature.

So convinced was I of their closeness that I decided to release them together that autumn. My hunch was that Trudy, after eighteen months of association with me and with Andre, would be "imprinted" by humankind and the special relationship with Andre.

I was wrong about that. I gave them their freedom on a chill November afternoon. Trudy surfaced once and looked back at me on the seawall. Then the gray water closed over her.

Andre returned a few days later, alone. I never saw Trudy again.

As far as resolving Andre's life was concerned, I was back where I'd started from. It wasn't until a few years later that I learned I needn't have worried. The testimony of a number of reliable witnesses assured me that the poetic saying "Love will find a way" extends to sealdom.

Al Eaton, the unofficial guardian of Rockport's waterfront, hailed me one June morning. He offered this earthy report: "I got some news for you, Harry, and you better believe it! A few days back, I came down as I do to look things over. Well, sir, I looked down over the seawall and there's Andre with a female. He was topside, a-huggin' her with his flippers and puttin' it right to her. A one-night stand, I suppose. Haven't seen the lady since."

There were a number of witnesses to Andre's conquest, fortunately all of a tolerant bent. How Andre had managed to lure a nubile lady from the outer ledges to such a public trysting place I will never know. I was quite aware that harbor seals will mate either on land or at sea, but I much doubt that many seal cows have been serviced on a marina float.

I was too delighted with Al's news to waste good time pondering an imponderable. And I discounted Susan's romantic suggestion that Andre had brought his girlfriend home to meet the family.

The wonderful bond between seal and man. (Lew Dietz)

Andre liked to frolic at liberty in Rockport Harbor (left). It was a long, hard winter when Andre was confined to Luke Allen's boat shed. Here he looks wistfully out to sea (below). (Jim Moore)

11

Mysteries

Thinking back, I realize that in those first years I'd regarded Andre much as I had all the other wild creatures I'd harbored in the course of my life. I found him interesting and fun. My attitude might be characterized as one of amused affection. Something happened in the late fall of 1967 that altered—and, at the same time, added a new dimension to—our relationship.

Andre had been a pleasure; now, suddenly, he became a source of wonder.

My boyhood days had been filled with wonder. My young mind had been stirred by a thousand questions for which I had no answers. Maturity hasn't diluted my wonder. I am quite willing to accept the probability that there are questions that will forever remain unanswered, but certainly there are as well mysteries that science has made no real attempt to explain. If I could not find the answers, I might at least learn to ask the right questions.

What astonished me was Andre's sensory awareness.

There was this matter of his love affair with Aqua-Lungers. Let a diver enter the water, and Andre was there with him. So common were these instances that I had come to take them for granted. The events of that late fall afternoon shook me out of my complacency.

Four of us had set out in Howard Kimball's lobster boat to dive for scallops off Ram Island. Andre was dozing peacefully on Howard's float as we pushed off. Harbor seals, unlike their cousins, the otters and sea lions, have a highly developed capacity for doing nothing. Andre was still snoozing when the boat cleared the first point of land. It is four miles to Ram Island, which is well westward and out of sight of the inner harbor.

When we had arrived at the diving site and arranged our gear, Edgar Post, one of our complement, went overboard to look over the bottom. Edgar was submerged for no more than fifteen minutes. As he surfaced to report, I was startled to see a familiar whiskered face bobbing off the boat's transom.

I yelled, "Don't look now, but we have company!"

Edgar turned to come face-to-face with friend Andre.

Actually, the full import of this demonstration didn't hit me at once. I suppose I'd assumed that Andre's meeting up with scuba divers had been happenstance—that while cruising about he had stumbled upon them. The more I thought about it, the clearer it became that Andre had not just stumbled upon divers; he'd homed in on them. That day he had been four miles from the diving operation. Once Edgar had hit the water, Andre had come at top speed, unerringly, to the target.

That, I told myself, was something to think about. I had marveled at the sensitivity and fine tuning of Andre's five senses, but none of them could explain this exploit of long-range location and identification. I was forced to the conclusion that a harbor seal possessed some sense or employed some system outside the ken of modern science.

Toothed whales and porpoises communicate by ultrasonic whistles and locate and identify food by echolocation. There is evidence that some of the pinnipeds produce high-frequency pulses in water similar to those used by bats in the air. And yet there is no firm evidence that harbor seals have this capacity for echolocation, useful though it would be for short-range identification. But even an assumption of this capability would scarcely explain Andre's talent for locating and identifying an object four miles away.

Although its outer ears are closed when it is submerged, a seal is still able to hear. Sounds are registered along the tube that leads from the outer ear to the eardrum. Andre certainly is capable of picking up the sound of a scuba diver's air regulator and the throb of a boat's propeller; but even in view of the fact that water is a better conductor of sound than the air, it seemed to me highly unlikely that Andre was guided to a distant target by his ears.

I pondered this puzzle for some days. What I arrived at finally was more a hunch than an answer. My hunch, however, was supported by additional observations.

One May afternoon I had a vivid demonstration of Andre's "sixth sense." He was enjoying his recess in the harbor that day, frolicking in the water with little on his mind but expending his animal energy. He stopped to rest for a moment, assuming his typical natant position—eyes exposed, whiskers trailing in the water. Suddenly he stiffened. Normally, a harbor seal submerges slowly, as a submarine does, but when alerted he dives with a swift forward-thrusting motion. I saw the flash of his back as he went into a dive. He bobbed up seventy-five yards off with an alewife in his mouth.

The harbor surface had been spackled by a shoal of feeding mackerel. Andre is not fond of mackerel. He loves herring, and the alewife is a member of the herring family. To me, it was quite obvious that Andre's whiskers were tuned receptors, and that these vibrissae had picked up a message that had been transmitted to his brain. From a wide range of stimuli his trailing whiskers had informed him not only of the presence of fish some distance off, but his favorite fish.

It was quite obvious to me that the harbor seal's whiskers were important sensory structures. There had to be a good reason for such a prominent feature. Certainly, the cat doesn't wear whiskers to hide a scar or to satisfy its vanity: They serve to afford the cat a tactile awareness of its immediate environment. Surely, I conjectured, the harbor seal's elaborate adornment served a larger purpose, acting, perhaps, as both long- and short-range receptors.

I could find nothing in the scientific literature that offered a satisfying answer. Investigations conducted at the Stanford Research Institute, in which it was revealed that sea lions will pick up pieces of fish as quickly in total darkness as in daylight, appeared to indicate the use of active sonar. However, a Canadian authority (R. W. Dykes), after completing a study of the harbor seal's whiskers, concluded that it was unlikely that the vibrissae of this species serve as sensors in a biosonar system. Thus, the question of what the harbor seal's whiskers tell it remains largely unanswered.

While I marveled at Andre's sensory sophistication, I knew very well that he saw nothing extraordinary about his capabilities. Seals had been using such systems for a long time. Oddly, the United States alone had spent several billion dollars in the twenty-five years prior to World War II in solving the problems of echo sounding and underwater identification without giving serious thought to marine mammals that have been using systems for this purpose for 20 million years.

Although I arrived at no full and satisfactory answer to the questions Andre's exploits posed, the experience did throw light on something else that had been puzzling me. For a half-dozen years I'd observed a blind seal on the outer ledges. This sightless old matri-arch had produced a series of healthy pups, and appeared healthy herself and in no way hampered by her deficiency. The seal is one of those rare mammals that see equally well in the water or in the air, but that blind seal cow provided ample evidence that these marine mammals call upon senses other than their eyes in their search for food.

Among those who have observed animals at close range there is, I suppose, a temptation to overestimate the intelligence of nonhu-man creatures. It may well be, as some biologists would have it, that animals' lives are lived on the subconsciously reflexive level, and that all other manifestations of "thought" are no more than behavior, modified by experience to a creaturely form of cunning. I have never been tempted to get drawn into the profitless argument as to whether animals think or do not think. I will say only that on one occasion, Andre displayed an ingenuity that indicated—to me, at least—a capacity for reasoning.

Running out of my stock of frozen herring that October, a few weeks before Andre's scheduled release from his pen, I was forced to fall back on mackerel. I rowed out to the pound and set the bucket on the platform.

"Andre, old boy," I said, dumping the fish on the deck, "what I've got is mackerel, and you can take them or leave them."

Andre nudged the fish and snorted his disgust. He slapped one around a bit, finally ripping it open with his teeth and pushing it, untasted, into the water of the enclosure. The macerated mackerel sank to the bottom of the slatted pen.

He looked down at it idly for a few moments, sulking, I sup-pose. Suddenly, he slid into the water and took a position at the far end of his pen. I waited, curious to learn what the rascal was up to.

As I watched, Andre went into a steep dive. To my amazement, he popped up, not with the mackerel in his mouth but with a live harbor pollock.

Actually, I didn't immediately grasp what was going on. It wasn't until he mashed up a second and a third fish and shoved them into the water that it dawned on me that he was using those despised mackerel as chum to toll in through the slatted cage fish that he *did* like.

I rowed ashore a bit shaken. I don't know to what extent he refined the operation, but I do know he made good use of the frozen mackerel, for he appeared sleek and well fed when I released him in mid-November.

Afterward, I wondered if I should not have made a closer study of Andre's fishing operation. Perhaps it's just as well I didn't bring in a team of scientific observers. Andre has no high regard for skeptics. In a delicious fantasy I see him turning disdainfully to the circle of intent scholarly faces and saying, "So I use toll bait to catch fish. You think I'm stupid or something?"

The revelation of Andre's "reasoning" power opened my mind to new vistas. Lacking the funds and the training to set up elaborate controlled experiments, I decided I might at least search for practical applications of Andre's special talents. Not only would I satisfy my own curiosity, but perhaps I would perform a service for Andre as well.

As mentioned earlier, a sea otter is incapable of lazing around and doing nothing; a harbor seal feels no urge whatever to improve each shining hour. Over the years I had noted that my dogs enjoyed having a job to do. A trained hunting dog feels himself a cut above the tramp town dog. My departed retriever, Scamp, simply refused to associate with street mutts. As a pro, Scamp had her self-respect to maintain.

Perhaps I have a touch of Puritanism in me. Mistaken or not, I hold to the notion that a little work never hurt anyone. Although I had no wish to apply human standards to a seal, it did strike me that given a useful job, Andre might become less of a bum. One logical application of Andre's special talents was immediately obvious. In the past, I'd been called upon to dive for victims of drowning accidents. There was no question in my mind that Andre was better equipped than I to perform that unpleasant task.

A friend donated an oversize baby doll. As a preliminary test I tossed the weighted doll into the harbor and directed Andre to retrieve it. No problem. He was back in an instant, the "drowning victim" in his mouth. Next, I threw the doll in the water out of sight of Andre and, using a hand signal, said, "Go get it, Andre." Still no problem.

So far, so good. If Andre was to be useful, he would be called upon to retrieve at distant sites unfamiliar to him. Ben Allen was helping me at the time. We decided to transport the doll and Andre two miles to Camden Harbor. Earlier, I'd solved the logistical problem of transporting Andre's two-hundred-plus pounds by constructing a carrying cage. Together, we trucked Andre to Camden, hiding the doll behind the seat. I sank the doll in Camden Harbor while Andre was still in his cage. We lugged the cage to the float and released Andre.

Again, I said, "Go get it, Andre."

Without hesitation, he flipped himself overboard. In less than a minute Andre surfaced and came to us, the doll in tow.

I should have been satisfied. Hadn't I proved my point? I'd even gone so far as to test him with a larger figure, one the size of an eight-year-old child. His performance was more than satisfactory. Then I remembered that on several occasions I'd been called upon to search for bodies in a number of the many flooded limestone quarries in the area. How would Andre perform as my surrogate in such an assignment?

Certainly, Andre was welcome to that job. I didn't like diving in those forbidding waters. The walls are sheer, and some of those abandoned mines are 200 feet deep. I was particularly apprehensive in the winter when the quarries were frozen and it was necessary to cut a hole in the ice. I mentioned my uneasiness to Ben as we discussed the proposal in Andre's presence one afternoon.

"Well, what about it, old man?" I said, turning to Andre. "Swimming under ice shouldn't bother you any."

Andre gave me his usual inscrutable stare. I didn't expect any comment. Consulting with Andre is merely an exercise in civility. Ben and I decided to go ahead with the test the next day.

The following afternoon I brought down the carrying cage. Andre had never balked at entering the portable crate. Always he appeared to enjoy the ride, relaxing as majestically as some maharajah in his royal litter.

He refused that day. Swimming just offshore, he took one look at the crate we were carrying down to the rock and off he headed for the open sea. It was three days before he returned.

I didn't know quite what to think about his odd behavior. Certainly, I was reluctant to accept the "unnatural" implications of his actions. In any event, I decided to forget the quarry. And I might have dropped the matter entirely had it not been for a visit in the spring from Bob Cisson, a *National Geographic* magazine photographer.

With Cisson was Bob Horstman, who had brought up a harbor seal, and about whom Cisson had done a story. Horstman was looking for a young female seal and was hopeful that I might help him.

In the course of our discussion at Andre's pen, I mentioned his refusal to enter his cage on the day of the scheduled quarry experiment. Both men were interested, and offered to help me follow through on the test. I wasn't entertaining the notion that Andre had sensed my uneasiness about the quarry, but I was curious to learn how he would react to a strange situation.

I got my answer promptly enough. We carried Andre to the quarry and released him. There was something about that place he simply didn't care for. I tossed the doll into the water and directed him to retrieve it. He made a few shallow dives and struggled to get out. The doll is still there at the bottom of the quarry.

I never did come up with a satisfactory explanation for his behavior. I don't believe it was the depth of the water that bothered him. I've read accounts of the diving capabilities of some of the pinnipeds. Gray seals have been known to dive to depths of 500 feet, and a harp seal was netted at 600 feet. According to one authority (Gavin Maxwell), two bladdernosed seals were taken alive for the Bremerhaven Zoo at over 1,200 feet. Although I don't believe that harbor seals are deep divers, I'd seen my pup Basil descend to 90 feet and come up with bottom-feeding fish such as the sculpin.

Finally, all I had to fall back on was the possibility that Andre had picked up my feeling of uneasiness. In the course of that summer I had some further evidence to support that admittedly shaky theory.

One afternoon, I was diving in the harbor in search of a mooring. I'd descended to forty feet, which was not excessive, except that the water was murky that day. Diving in water when the visibility is down to a few feet can be spooky.

As I searched among the weeds and rocks in that eerie half-light, I began to feel a bit uneasy. I was about to kick to the surface when something took me from the rear. Under the best of circumstances a sudden assault in forty feet of water can curl your hair. Close to panic, I reached for my knife.

There was Andre, and he was in a state of high agitation. He nipped at my arm and then began tugging at my flippers. Quite obviously, he thought I was in danger, and he was telling me to get up out of that murky water. I was in no mood to argue with him. I surfaced quickly, Andre nagging at my heels. Once my panic had ebbed, my next emotion was anger, and that, too, quickly cooled, so obvious were his concern and relief.

I am a solitary walker. All that winter on my walks in the snow, I thought of Andre and the new direction of my interest. I realized that I had barely begun to explore his intelligence and capabilities. Our special relationship afforded me a unique opportunity. How many men were privileged to enjoy the complete trust of a wild creature over so long a period? It was time I began to consider a more serious approach to an understanding of this remarkable animal. I needed help.

A promise of help came out of the blue the following spring. I had a phone call from Walter Stone, director of the Franklin Park Zoo in Boston. He told me that Bio-Dynamics, Inc., a biological lab in Cambridge, Massachusetts, was embarking upon a behavioral study that would involve harbor seals. Dr. Stone wondered if I might be interested in working on the project. My immediate and unequivocal answer was that indeed, I would be interested.

12

Luigi

I had known Dr. Stone for a number of years. He had called on me one summer; actually, he'd come to see Andre, with the idea, I suspect, of winnowing fact from fiction in the newspaper accounts of Andre's adventures.

Walter was a lively and charming fellow, refreshingly atypical of the scientific-establishment breed. Whatever skepticism he may have had was quickly dissolved; wise and imperturbable Andre won him over completely. In fact, Walter confessed that he was a bit awed by Andre's intelligence and response to direction. Subsequently, he brought in a number of fellow zoologists to share his wonder.

We became good friends over the several years of our association (he died a few years ago in an auto accident). Always interested in gaining new knowledge of the natural world, I helped Walter collect avian specimens for the zoo. Together we visited the uninhabited islands in the bay, gathering both eggs and nestlings of cormorants, eider ducks, great black-backed gulls, and black guillemots, known on the Maine coast as sea pigeons. Of all these marine species, only the guillemots made nests that were difficult to locate; in fact, the outer islands were so plastered with nests of other species that one had to walk gingerly to avoid stepping on eggs.

Black-backed gulls, once relatively rare on our coast, had increased to a point where they'd become an ecological detriment. Larger and more aggressive than herring gulls, the black-backs preyed on other species, destroying eggs and young.

On these expeditions with Walter I noted the eider duck's extremely effective method of protecting its eggs. Upon intrusion, a setting bird would evacuate its nest and its intestines at the same instant, rendering the eggs both unrecognizable and uninviting.

Although we searched diligently, we were still without guillemots. My son Steve was with us one day as we continued our fruitless search.

"What are you looking for?" Steve asked Walter.

"A guillemot nest," Walter told him.

"Why didn't you say so?" Steve said. "I'll find you a guillemot nest."

And this he proceeded to do. As a boy he had spent part of a summer on Kent's Island in the Bay of Fundy with Professor Charles Huntington, of Maine's prestigious Bowdoin College, who is credited with locating the secret nesting places of the stormy petrel. The professor that summer had been collecting guillemot eggs. Unlike the gulls and eiders that nest in the open, the guillemots secrete their nests deep in dark rock crevices. In short order, Steve supplied Walter with the specimens he required.

To top off these expeditions, Walter usually insisted on taking me out to dinner. He had a rather endearing habit of trying to get me stiff on martinis, and my attitude to this can best be illustrated by a story they tell around the village about Eben Calderwood. A fellow citizen waylaid Eben on the way to town one Saturday night and asked him where he was bound. "Well," said Eben, "I understand that Willy Churchill cal'lates to get me drunk, and I cal'late to fall right into his plans."

One night Walter almost caused our waitress to drop the tray that carried our third round of drinks. He was using his jacket pocket as an incubator for a guillemot egg. The baby bird chose that moment to peck out of its shell and land in an empty glass.

"I do prefer olives in my martinis," Walter informed the waitress, "but I'll let it go this time."

As good as his word, Walter set up the meeting in Boston with the Bio-Dynamics brass. I had little idea of what it was they wanted from me, and I wasn't much more enlightened when the meeting was over. All Walter had told me on the phone was that the lab was looking for someone who knew something about harbor seals, and who might be able to train them for specific tasks. I was curious to know more specifically the nature of the project, but I refrained from pressing them for fear of betraying my eagerness to have at long last some support for my investigations.

Over coffee, I did say that if they wanted me to go ahead, I'd have to know within a few weeks, because training for specific tasks would call for a seal pup, and the whelping season was upon us.

Finally, the head man did ask me a specific question. Could I train a harbor seal to respond to radio signals when the seal was out of sight of its control? I said no one seems to know much about the harbor seal's sensory equipment, but I was sure that, given time, this could be accomplished. The meeting broke up with a promise that I would hear from them soon.

I did hear from Dr. Charles Budrose, the firm's assistant technical director of behavioral research. In a memo, Dr. Budrose attempted to structure the training program, listing the "behaviors" he considered desirable:

1) To have the animal locate and retrieve a floating object

2) To train the animal to search for and tag a floating object

3) To train the animal to search for and tag a submerged object

4) To train the animal to deposit a package at a specific point;

5) For all the above, to determine whether the animal could perform under adverse weather conditions; and

6) To train the animal to find a school of fish.

Dr. Budrose concluded by writing that he knew very little about the learning capabilities of harbor seals, a statement that was self-evident. Train a seal to find a school of fish, indeed! How, I wondered, did Dr. Budrose think seals had managed to survive for 20 million years? Nor did the other "behaviors" present any great challenge. Andre had demonstrated most of these capabilities time and time again.

In the course of the next several weeks, exchanges of letters began to bring into focus the practical applications the program was designed to explore. Each year, a fortune in tools was dropped overboard from marine installations such as oil rigs. Could a harbor seal be trained to retrieve such tools? In Alaska, storms took their toll on expensive king crab traps, tearing them from their buoys. Could a seal be trained to locate these lost traps and buoy them?

I replied to Dr. Budrose that, given time and sufficient funding, a harbor seal might very well be trained for these and a hundred other underwater assignments. Actually, I was reasonably certain that these tasks were well within the range of a harbor seal's capabilities, but at this stage of negotiations, I was reluctant to confess how simple I thought it would be. I was anxious to begin.

I "acquired" pup Luigi the morning of May 18, roughly two days after his birth on the outer ledges, appropriating him, I told myself, in the interest of science, and in the hope of narrowing the gap of ignorance that lay between man and this misunderstood marine mammal. By then an old hand as a surrogate mother, I weaned Luigi in ten days and had him ready to go to work for his board.

Luigi began his training June 18, exactly one month after his capture. In three days he was retrieving lines and objects both floating and submerged. I used a white ear syringe that would float when empty and sink when filled. In a week he was retrieving, as well, a doll sunk in fifteen feet of water.

The lab had supplied me with a short piece of board fixed with a snap hook to which a buoyed length of line could be attached, the idea being that the seal would be trained to snap a line to some submerged object so that it might be salvaged. Willing and eager though Luigi was, this rig was a bit too heavy for so young a seal. I called in Andre, who, with the casual ease of an old pro, demonstrated to the young novitiate how the task should be accomplished.

As I had suspected, these simple and potentially useful jobs presented no great challenge, even to a month-old harbor seal. True, I had perfected certain training techniques, but the success was largely a demonstration of the seal's natural capabilities, intelligence, and, even more important, eagerness to oblige.

My waterfront friends were no more than casually beguiled by my new interest. They dismissed my eccentricities with the thought that a fellow who played with seals for fun and climbed trees for a living couldn't be all bad. Visiting yachtsmen, on the other hand, were totally unprepared for what they came upon in Rockport Harbor. I would hail a boat as it approached the marina and ask the crew if someone would mind accepting a line from a seal.

"Accept a line from a *what?*" was the usual incredulous response.

As soon as I made it clear that I wasn't pulling their collective legs, visiting yachtsmen, although understandably bemused, were all too happy to assist. I would dispatch Luigi with the line. He would deliver it and return to me for further instructions. It is safe to say that taking a line from a harbor seal was a unique experience for these seagoing vacationers, and one that served them as a conversation piece for some years to come.

These daily training sessions ran for two hours at the most. I feared that pushing a young seal too fast might result in stress; nor did I release Luigi in the outer harbor, knowledge of the presence of great white sharks and the memory of Basil's violent end being still fresh in my mind. By fall, Luigi would have gained enough size and maturity to fend better for himself.

In early June, I wrote to Charles Budrose. "At present," I reported, "I am concentrating on improving Luigi's performance of the tasks he has learned. These and other more-complicated assignments will be attempted in strange waters when he is four months hold. His main problem at present is his wariness of strangers. At first, he would take a line to a strange boat and when someone reached out to accept the line, he would panic and return to me. After a period of schooling, he came to realize that his job was to 'hand' the line to a stranger. This he will now do under most circumstances. He will deliver the line, return to me, and then upon direction go back to the boat and bring me the line. This seal must be observed to be appreciated, so I urge you to come to Maine and see for yourself as soon as possible."

Despite my urging, Budrose did not appear on the scene, but my friend Walter Stone arrived in late June to observe and monitor the program for his own interest. What he saw prompted him to send a memo to Budrose, importuning his colleague to make the trip. "I was frankly amazed at what Harry has accomplished with such a young animal," Walter wrote. "I think his progress to date would certainly indicate that the project should be continued, and will attract the interest of funding agencies. It would seem to me at the present time it would be difficult to determine the limits within which a seal can be trained, although they are quite obviously broad. It may be a little difficult to keep ahead of the seal."

It became clear to me by then that Bio-Dynamics was on a fishing expedition, and without any specific purpose in mind but testing the harbor seal's potential, with the hope of finding funding from private or federal sources. They were leaving it up to me to develop procedures and possible applications for the harbor seal's special talents.

And by that time my mind was fairly exploding with possibilities. I envisioned Andre on a rescue mission carrying a breeches-buoy line from the shore to a stranded vessel. I could see him salvaging storm-lost lobster traps along our own coast. I could see a whole elite corps of trained harbor seals carrying messages to and from divers, or protecting sensitive underwater installations.

Sadly, as my interest waxed, the interest of my sponsor appeared to wane. I could only guess that the hoped-for funding didn't materialize. As fall approached I had to consider the problem of Luigi's winter quarters, if the project was to continue. I wrote that I needed a firm commitment if I was to carry on beyond the summer.

Budrose did come up in late September and expressed satisfaction with Luigi's progress. He told me he would send up a young man to observe my training procedures and return to Boston with the seal, which had been a part of our original agreement.

The young man arrived one dreary November day. He was to be the seal-handler, he told me. Luigi would be installed at the New England Aquarium, and he would work with him there. Would I show him what I had done with Luigi?

This I did without too much grace. He seemed excessively

uninterested in my training procedures, and even less interested in their scientific implications. He packed up my little seal and took him by truck to Boston.

I received final payment for my work in February, at which time I wrote that I hoped to continue the project in the spring, but would withhold details of my plans pending word from them.

I had no further word; nor, so far as I was ever able to ascertain, was further work done with Luigi at the aquarium. Although he was given the best of care, he died four years later. I never did learn the details; I can only suppose he died of boredom.

13

Jesse

Although by the winter's end I'd given up hope of funding for my seal investigations, I continued to have some wild and heady thoughts about my elite "seal corps." Even if I'd had the necessary training, I lacked the means to invest in the expensive equipment needed to enter the dominion of pure science. But with Andre's guidance I could at least demonstrate that the neglected harbor seal possessed a wide range of natural talents that modern man's gadgetry was unlikely ever to match.

I thought about the mlllions the government had spent locating and retrieving the atomic bomb lost a few years ago off the coast of Spain. I had no doubt that Andre and his fellows could have located and buoyed the bomb for a bucket of raw fish.

Certainly, other marine mammals might be trained to aid man, but none is so ideally fitted for use on seagoing assignments. The bottle-nosed porpoise (dolphin) is not fond of cold water; the harbor seal's water-temperature tolerance is broad. Transporting a porpoise is a major undertaking, requiring a special tank and lifting gear; a harbor seal can be taken cross-country in a plane or the front seat of a car and can remain out of water almost indefinitely.

The sea lion, smart as it is, has distinct disadvantages. A sea lion is restive and naturally flamboyant, and its raucous barking would negate its usefulness in a sensitive assignment; the harbor seal is relaxed and relatively silent. Like the porpoise, the sea lion doesn't adapt well to cold water. Moreover, at least two years are required to train a sea lion; a harbor seal matures earlier and can be fully trained within a year. One of the most important advantages the harbor seal has over other marine mammals is its size; at a maximum weight of around 250 pounds, the harbor seal is one–third to one-half the size of most other members of the seal family. Perhaps most important, I had proved that a harbor seal thrives in association with man, and can be trained in its natural habitat.

My excursions into scientific byways did nothing to alter my close association with Andre. Although I had that winter abandoned regular feedings when I discovered that Andre was growing fat and sleek on his own foraging, we continued to meet and socialize every other day or so. He would come into the harbor through the ice floes, looking for me, so I made a point of checking the waterfront several times a day. If I spotted him, I'd give him a hail and he'd swim in to say hello. Some days, I would see him hauled out on Howard Kimball's wharf, and I'd drive around and spend some time with him. Although the winter was a lonely time for Andre, he appeared to be reasonably well adjusted to living in his two worlds.

In these, his middle years, Andre had achieved a sage maturity. His attitude toward me had changed subtly from a filial attachment to one of avuncular indulgence. I'm sure I tried his vast patience, particularly in my efforts to make him a useful member of society.

I had been made particularly aware of this the summer before, when I was busy with Luigi's training. He didn't mind showing Luigi how to put a snap hook on some object, but when I tried to put a light harness collar on him to be used on those occasions when a heavy line was to be carried out to a vessel, he made it quite clear that I had gone a bit far. Andre looked at the rig in disgust and simply refused to wear it.

I coaxed him. I remonstrated with him. No sale: He flatly refused to oblige. Finally, I slammed the harness on the deck and went ashore in a huff with the bucket of fish I'd brought for his supper.

Once ashore, I regretted my childish behavior. After all, a harness was a badge of servitude, and as such, an affront to Andre's dignity. I jumped into the boat and returned to the pound. There I found Andre waiting in portly majesty, the harness over his neck. Apparently he'd decided not to make an issue of the silly business; if wearing the harness meant that much to me, he'd indulge my whim. Besides, he wanted his fish. You may be sure he got his supper, and never again did I ask him to wear a harness.

In my wildest flights of fancy, the thought of training harbor seals for use in tactical warfare never entered my mind. Prior to World War I, a Russian scientist named Durov had succeeded in training seals for rescue work, and in the process realized he had the makings of a secret weapon. A seal fixed with a warhead that could detonate on contact could be dispatched on a kamikaze mission to destroy an enemy vessel. Once he had developed the device, Durov learned that both the Russians and British were interested in his invention. He couldn't bring himself to betray his seal friends whose trust he had worked so long to gain. He destroyed his plans.

By February, when I had about decided to relax and enjoy my easy and undemanding relationship with Andre, I received a cryptic letter from the US Navy Office of Naval Research.

"Dear Mr. Goodridge," the letter read. "It would appear that some of your interests would coincide with programs presently under the cognizance of this office. In order for a more complete evaluation of your past accomplishments and plans, we would appreciate a somewhat detailed letter, which due to its proprietary nature, should be sent by registered mail, so that we may more fully appreciate the present situation. This could well provide a basis for continued discussions or perhaps a visit to Maine or here in Washington, D.C." The curious and unsolicited letter gave me pause.

The writer, who identified himself as the agency's program director, Oceanic Biology Programs, had for reasons beyond my grasp taken great pains not to breathe a word of the nature of our mutual interest. Never before had I been beckoned down the dark corridors of clandestine Washington, and the invitation made me a bit uneasy.

Since I couldn't imagine what interest other than harbor seals we possibly could have in common, I came right out with it. I replied (via registered mail) that I assumed he had harbor seals in mind. I told him further that to write a letter detailing my accomplishments in this area would take more time than I could spare, but that I would be more than happy to meet with him at his convenience and discuss the matter.

I received a reasonably prompt reply in which my contact wrote, "We are indeed interested in your work with harbor seals. We, therefore, look forward to talking with you, at a day and time of your convenience, perhaps during the week of 7 April."

I called the Washington number he had given me and set up an appointment. Since the navy had spent millions developing underwater detection devices with hardly a sidelong glance at harbor seals, I wasn't at all surprised that no mention was made of paying the expenses of a seal fancier for the trip. I flew to Washington late in March at my own expense.

The complications involved in gaining an audience with my

ONR correspondent did nothing to ease my anxiety. After being cleared at the main reception center, I was directed across the street and through a guarded gate. When finally I located the proper office in the labyrinth of corridors, a secretary advised me that the director was ready to see me. He turned out to be a youngish, unprepossessing fellow of medium build and a vague, slightly harassed demeanor.

In the course of the brief amenities, I learned that he knew very little about seals, that his field was fish, and the specimens tucked around the small office confirmed his major interest. Curiously, though he recalled our correspondence, he seemed unsure of just why I was there. I got the impression that he thought it was *I* who wanted something from *him.*

With the idea of disabusing him of this notion, I went straight to the point. "Am I correct in my impression that the navy has not as yet developed a device with the capability of locating and identifying an underwater swimmer?"

Frowning, he nodded. "That is correct."

"Well," I said, "I've got such a device."

His eyes reflected cautious interest. "You have?"

"Yes, I have. What I have in mind is a harbor seal."

"Oh," he said.

I proceeded to support my thesis, giving him a brief account of my experiences with Andre, with special emphasis on his eerie talent for locating and identifying divers at long range. I could see that my contact was highly skeptical. This was indeed interesting, he admitted, but such observations did not constitute acceptable scientific proof. The implication was that an amateur should not be messing around in such arcane matters.

I resisted the impulse to point out to him that he was the one who had suggested that I make a six-hundred-mile trip in order to brief him on my "accomplishments." However, I did find myself overracting to his skepticism.

"Perhaps I can come up with acceptable scientific proof. My seal Andre will have to be confined in a week until November. I'll acquire a seal pup and train him specifically for this project, using any criteria you suggest."

I must say my contact was a credit to his profession: He wouldn't commit himself or his office without further information and evaluation. He would only say that he would be interested in the results of such a program. I departed with his promise that he would let me know "prior to a visit by this office or one of our scientific colleagues."

Returning to Maine from that never-never land of official Washington was like returning to Earth from the moon. I had received no commitment or solid encouragement, only a sort of dismissive promise of continued interest. Sensibly, I should have scrubbed the whole proposition and returned gratefully to my carefree amateur status. Instead, I decided to have a go at tilting with windmills. I wasn't so quixotic as to think that I could win over the navy brass with a breakthrough of an earthshaking nature, but at least I could prove that harbor seals were one hell of a lot smarter than some government-subsidized scientists.

On May 18, I captured a two-day-old harbor seal. I named him Jesse, and a gay and bright little fellow he was. In ten days flat, Jesse was weaned and ready to go to work. He would be trained as a specialist to identify and locate divers at long range.

In order to set up controlled experiments, I needed help. I contacted Ronn Young, a friend and fellow diver, and asked him if he'd act as my assistant. Ronn's regular employment was at night, and he was delighted to give me a hand during the days when I needed him.

Using the same white ear syringe I'd used in Luigi's training, I began what I considered to be a controlled experiment. First, I trained little Jesse to retrieve at short and then longer distances. Once I'd established in the pup's mind that the syringe was the token with which he'd be dealing, I had Ronn enter the water out of sight of Jesse, with the syringe in his possession. I would then direct Jesse to find the diver and return with the syringe. The syringe served as the proof that Jesse had made underwater contact with the hidden diver. At two months, pup Jesse was locating Ronn at distances of 100 yards and returning with the syringe.

I used the code word *attack* to trigger Jesse. Alert and eager, he would be swimming around near shore and awaiting my orders. I would give Ronn time to drive to the outer harbor and enter the water at some location unknown even to me. I'd say, "Jesse, a diver has entered the water out there someplace. Find him. Attack!"

It was beautiful to watch him respond. His head would pop up as he awaited the command. At the word *attack* he'd arch into the water and be gone. He went to the target at top speed and nothing diverted him from his mission. He was looking for a scuba diver, and a scuba diver he located in a matter of minutes. He would return to me with the syringe in his teeth.

Actually, Ronn had two syringes in his possession on most of these occasions. Once Jesse returned to me with the first syringe, I'd send him out again for the second. Although Ronn would move to a new location, my first thought was that Jesse would make a faster round-trip on the second run, since he had established the general target area on the first. This was not the case, however. Seldom was there an appreciable difference in elapsed time. This amounted to pretty fair proof that Jesse's orientation systems were fully auto-matic—that foreknowledge of a target area was not a factor in performance.

The two syringes once caused Jesse a bit of confusion.

One day in late July Ronn returned, chuckling. "I was swimming at around three fathoms when Jesse appeared. He grabbed the first syringe and started back, full clip. Suddenly, he swung around with sort of a double take. He'd seen that second syringe. I usually had it hidden, but this time I'd neglected to hide it. I could almost see his mind working: 'Hey, there's two of the danged things this trip.' He tried to grab the second one, and the first popped to the surface. He shot up to get that one, and then lost it trying to get both in his teeth. It was quite a circus. Finally, he said to hell with it and went back with one. By that time I was so doubled up laughing, I had to surface to pull myself together."

In the course of these sessions I discovered that Jesse required an interval of rest between missions. When he'd returned with the first syringe, he wouldn't respond at once to my command to go back to Ronn. He'd swim around me for several minutes until he felt he was ready to dive. I was a bit irritated until I realized that after an underwater sprint, he needed time to recover and "recharge his batteries." Once he had recovered, he needed no further urging; he was off in a flash.

Then, on the first day of August, Jesse failed to return from a mission. I knew at once that I'd made the mistake of feeding him too much. A fish was his reward for a successful mission, and my overfeeding had relaxed his motivation. As had Andre in his early years, Jesse had gone off on an excursion. I was hopeful that he'd return after a brief recess, but after ten days passed and he didn't appear, I sadly wrote him off as a casualty.

Eighteen days from the time of his departure, Jesse reappeared. I was overjoyed to see him, but my delight couldn't match Jesse's elation at the reunion. Never before had I seen a seal demonstrate such affection. He cuddled up to me and kept nipping at my arm as if to say, "Golly, it's sure great to be home!"

So back to work we went. Little Jesse had matured amazingly in those few weeks. It was obvious that he'd learned to fish for himself, for he was in fine physical shape; in fact, it was several days before I could get him to accept my frozen stock. His experience in the wild had improved his performance and increased his confidence, and I had no hesitation in stiffening the tests and sending him out on longer and longer missions.

His continued perfect scoring at identifying and locating distant divers convinced me that I had conclusive proof that a harbor seal employs some sense or combination of senses not as yet understood. I didn't discount the strong possibility that Jesse, once close to his target, homed in on the sound of a diver's air regulator. I wondered how he would score if I eliminated that sound source.

One day, I sent Ronn down without his air tank, equipped only with faceplate and snorkel. When Jesse went straightaway to the target and returned in minutes with the syringe, I knew I had proved what I'd set out to prove: that a harbor seal possessed a sixth sense, the nature of which warranted further investigation.

After my work with Jesse, I was confident that a harbor seal could not only identify and locate a diver at long distances, but could also be trained quite easily to neutralize the diver by removing his faceplate or flippers. I had had no communication with the ONR office since a letter in May confirming its interest in my investigations. Assuming the office was serious, I sent a report late in August. After a brief résumé of my experiments and conclusions, I made a blunt pitch for some action at the navy's end. I wrote that with fall coming on, I soon would have to turn Jesse loose, and that I hoped someone would be dispatched to Rockport to observe and evaluate my program.

No response. When Jesse disappeared again in early

September, I was just as pleased that no date had been set up. But again Jesse returned, this time in eleven days. And as before, Jesse demonstrated joy at being home and an eagerness to go to work. Although obviously Jesse didn't see anything mysterious or complicated about locating a diver several miles off, he did appear to delight in playing the hunting game.

However, from my point of view, I'd gone about as far as I could go with this program without research assistance. With my knowledge, but without any special urging on my part, several summer friends with navy connections did write the ONR office in an attempt to get some action, or at least to learn the reasons for the lack of it.

I can only conjecture that it was as a result of these promptings that I received a phone call from a Lieutenant Robert Ballard in early November. He planned to check in at Rockport to observe my program.

Bob Ballard turned out to be a friendly and practical fellow whose specialty with the navy had been the training of marine mammals. He'd had considerable success with dolphins, but very little experience with seals. He assured me that he had an open mind, and was eager to see what I'd done with young Jesse.

We foregathered at the Rockport waterfront that gray and chilly November morning—Ronn Young, the lieutenant, and I. I explained the setup.

"Let's assume that out there in the outer harbor somewhere is a secret underwater installation requiring maximum security. The navy doesn't want a diver in the area, not even an innocent curiosity seeker."

Ballard nodded. "I'll buy that."

"Okay," I said. "You don't have a detection device. What you do have is a harbor seal. Unknown to Jesse, I'll send a diver—Ronn here—to enter the water with this syringe. You name the place."

Ballard looked out to sea. "Look, I don't want to be ridiculous; I want to be reasonable."

"Go ahead, be ridiculous," I told him. "Jesse won't mind."

Shrugging, Ballard indicated a location in the outer harbor around a jut of land and more than a quarter–mile from where we stood.

"Right," I agreed, and nodded to Ronn. "You drive around by land, put on your scuba gear, and enter the water with the syringe. We'll give you twenty minutes."

Ronn hopped into his car and was off. I checked my watch, and Ballard and I pushed out in a boat to Jesse's pen. The little pup was alert and eager. It was apparent he knew there was something special about this mission.

When twenty minutes had passed, there was no need for me to tell Jesse his job. He had been trained as a specialist. His mysterious sensors would tell him when and where a diver had entered the water of the outer harbor. His training would tell him what he was expected to do.

I simply opened the pen gate. "Attack!" I said.

In a flash, Jesse rolled into a dive and was off. We both waited, my eyes on my watch, Ballard's to seaward. In three minutes flat, Jesse's head broke the surface of the water. The white syringe was in his mouth.

Ballard gasped. He stood there a moment, shaking his head. He said, incredulously, "I've never seen anything like that in my life!"

When he left for Washington that afternoon, Ballard was still shaking his head. "You'll hear from us," he said.

I never heard from Ballard or from the Office of Naval

Research. I learned later that the lieutenant had been transferred shortly after his trip to Maine. I made no further effort to continue the contact; I had proved my point, but, more than that, I had enjoyed with little Jesse one of the most unforgettable interludes of my life.

I had decided at the start that Jesse would not be consigned to an aquarium; he would be returned to the open sea from whence he had come. After his two ventures into the wild, surely he knew the things a young seal should know to survive. What he had learned from his association with man wouldn't help him or, I fervently hoped, hurt him. So I said good-bye and good luck to Jesse that day in late November. I sent him off and took up the pound that had been his Rockport summer home.

There was no way I could explain to him that he belonged not with me but on the outer ledges, nor did I know how to thank him for his company and his freely given help. Little Jesse returned several days later, looking for his pen. Not finding it, he departed for what I thought was the last time. And when I had no glimpse of him that winter, I was certain he had found his way back to where he truly belonged.

I was to see Jesse one more time. On June 18 of the following spring, he came swimming into the harbor to look over his old haunts. He responded to the sound of my voice when I greeted him, and he swam freely into his pen. Earlier, I had learned from Andre that harbor seals recognize a friend by the smell of his hair, so I bent low so that he might sniff my head. This he did, and he seemed satisfied that he was with a friend.

Rockport Harbor had not changed, but it was no longer home to little Jesse. He refused the thawed fish I offered. He'd become accustomed to fresh fish won by his own wiles in the open bay. I kept him a week, and when he continued to refuse the dead fish from my freezer, I let him go.

He didn't return, and so far as I can be certain, I never have seen him since then, though now and again in the open bay, I come upon a friendly harbor seal who seems to show more than a passing interest in me and my boat. Always, I turn away, feeling that it is best for both of us that things be left as they are.

Harry learned from Andre that seals recognize friends by the smell of their hair. (Lew Dietz)

14

The Old Mariner

The winter of 1972 was another buster. The ordeal wasn't so much in the depth of snow as it was the unrelenting cold. Bitter nights locked the harbor in ice, at times so thick a man could cross on it from shore to shore.

I didn't see too much of Andre, needless to say. He no longer relied on me for food, so there was no necessity for him to challenge the ice. During the brief periods when a channel opened up, he'd check in for a spell, then return to the open sea.

Where he went for periods of two or three weeks, I never knew. I assumed these voyages took him to far places, for I would have had reports of sightings had he remained in the Penobscot Bay area. Andre by then was as well known along this piece of coast as Senator Ed Muskie. I was concerned, but not worried unduly: Andre was mature and in his prime, seasoned, wise, and resourceful. I began to think of my friend Andre as the Old Mariner.

Not that Andre was old in terms of a harbor seal's life expectancy, though what that may be is only a guess. A harbor seal in a Tacoma, Washington, aquarium died in 1974 at the age of thirty-three. And one of a pair of Maine harbor seals at the Dallas Aquarium died when he was in his mid-twenties. Whether the normal life span of a harbor seal in its natural habitat is more or less than this is a moot question. Certainly, Andre showed no signs of physical deterioration. If these were his middle years, he wore them well.

I had no doubt that he had met up with his fellows on these journeys. What I didn't know and wondered about was how he was received in the wild kingdom. Were his scars of battle no worse than wild bull seals incur and carry as testimony of honorable battle, or was this strange wanderer an object of mockery, a pariah to avoid. Perhaps, because of his obvious "difference," he was treated as a sage, a cut above the ruck of sealdom. For the most part, harbor seals are solitary hunters, but did he haul out on the ledges with his kind to rest and bask? Although I had no way of knowing, my feeling was that he did not. My hunch was that Andre knew he was different, and the knowing made him a loner. His difference lay in the fact that he needed people more than he needed seals.

There could be no doubt of his need for human company, for he came home whenever the harbor was ice–free. And one unforgettable day he came with escort, and in a style befitting an arriving potentate.

That day in mid-February the local fishermen had called for the Coast Guard icebreaker *Swivel* to clear a channel through the harbor ice. Howard Kimball was in his yard working on gear when he saw the vessel clear the point. He went down to the end of his wharf to wave his thanks and greetings. The skipper returned the salute through the wheelhouse window, and then, yelling something barely audible above the thunder of buckling ice, he shoved his thumb sternward.

"Gorry, I couldn't believe my eyes," Howard told me later. "There was old Andre in the icebreaker's wake. He was putting on quite a show, porpoising over the ice cakes and all but taking bows.

I swear, he acted like that icebreaker had been sent over to clear the harbor for *him*."

Once the ice had gone in the spring, Andre spent most of his time in the harbor. After the lonely winter, the spring activity was a godsend. Andre was right there in the thick of it when the boats were put over and floats put out. The day the Boat Club float was towed into position, Andre hopped aboard for a free ride and then fussed around as the chains were hooked up and the ramp jockeyed into place. He was in the way, of course, but all hands tolerated his officious supervision.

After all, Andre was the town's honorary harbormaster, a title that had been bestowed upon him a few years earlier by the then town manager, Bob Steele, at the suggestion of a number of the local citizenry. If truth be told, I was the one who had made the original suggestion in an unguarded moment. I lacked the wit to realize that as the *official* harbormaster, I'd be duty–bound to see to it that my honorary deputy observed the waterfront rules and courtesies like any commoner. When Andre continued to do as he pleased, and more and more assumed the prerogatives of an elder statesman, I found myself in an uncomfortable position.

A few days before Andre was to go into the protective custody of his pen, I had a visit from the town constable. He was miffed. He wished to use his dinghy to get out to his boat, and Andre refused to vacate it. Moreover, I was informed, when his boy attempted to move Andre, my seal had nipped the lad's hat from his head and flung it overboard.

Together, we trekked down to the waterfront to straighten out the matter. Sure enough, there was the honorary harbormaster in full possession of the constable's dinghy. As I was rousting Andre out of the boat, I spotted the boy's hat drifting out to sea.

"Okay," I said to Andre, "you tossed that hat overboard; now you go get it and bring it here."

Still smarting at having his siesta disturbed, Andre snorted his displeasure, but he did streak out and return with the hat. He delivered it to me and I handed it to the constable. Not entirely mollified, the constable muttered his thanks, feeling, no doubt, that to do any less in the circumstance would have been boorish.

Andre went into his pen in mid-May, and I was able to put off making any major decision about his future. He appeared to be reconciled to this curtailment of his freedom, but I noted that when the crowds began to gather in the summer, Andre was beginning to lose his early zest for showmanship. As always, he enjoyed the attention, but his eagerness to please all those people in shorts was noticeably absent. He would go through the business as directed, but like that of an actor in a long-running play on Broadway, his performance was perfunctory.

And I must say, I too was beginning to tire of the old routine. Even an incorrigible ham may reach a point where audiences cease to stimulate him. The problem was that the crowds, which once numbered in the scores, now gathered by the hundreds. Many of them came from long distances, and since there was no way I could abruptly terminate the summer routine without disappointing a lot of people, I continued putting on these free performances. I was a bit irked now and then when someone in the crowd would complain when Andre refused to give his best effort.

I might say, "Sorry about tonight's show, folks. If you'd care to go to the box office, your money will be refunded."

In the course of a summer I could expect a dozen or more calls from wealthy summer people on the islands. They were coming over with a boatload of guests; could I assure them that Andre would appear? My stock reply was that I had to feed Andre at seven, so I would be there. That was my way of saying that the kind of show it would be was up to Andre.

And of course there were the campaigning politicians forever on the lookout for a ready-made audience, and mindful that an office-seeker could do worse than have his picture taken with a seal. A few years after his last run for the presidency, Adlai Stevenson dropped by to see Andre. After the show he commented upon Andre's loyal constituency, adding that doubtless seal Andre could have made a better run for the highest office than he had.

Something that happened in the course of that summer confirmed my feeling that Andre had learned a thing or two on his journeys in the savage world beyond the harbor. That was the Summer of the Bluefish in Maine. These battling game fish hadn't appeared in our waters in the memory of the living. The run began in late June, when big blues—ten- to fifteen-pounders—struck in along our coast, and everyone and his brother geared up and set out for them. The blues would take a variety of spoons and plugs, as well as live bait; in fact, they would hit at anything moving when they were in a feeding frenzy. There is no more voracious fish in the sea than a big blue. They have razor-sharp teeth and powerful jaws, and when they slash into a shoal of menhaden, the water turns red with the carnage.

The appearance of the blues in our waters wasn't entirely a boon. They drove every other species of fish out to sea. I had a hard time finding prime fish for Andre, so when I boated four good blues one day, I decided to share my luck with my friend.

I kept the fish hidden until after I'd fed him a few poor herring; then I produced a blue from the boat and held it up for his appreciation. The appreciation was not forthcoming. The only word to describe Andre's reaction was panic. He backed off and plunged into his pool. When he surfaced I tossed the fish onto his platform and attempted to reassure him. Finally, he approached the fish and shoved it gingerly with his nose, but it was a good five minutes before he got up the courage to take it in his teeth.

I realized then the reason for his strange behavior. Clearly, he had met up with these sea marauders in his travels. No doubt, he had joined in the hunt when the blues were in a feeding frenzy, and the slashing he'd gotten had been stored indelibly in his memory.

Andre did finally feast on that blue, but not before he'd made a show of his valor, swimming about with it in his mouth, tossing it into the air, and showing off outrageously.

Andre's failing enthusiasm for pleasing crowds in no way affected his ready willingness to give me a hand when I had need of his special talents. There was one afternoon when I was working on his pen and lost my hammer overboard. I roused Andre from his nap and pointed at the water. "Go get it, Andre," I directed.

Andre had no idea what it was I'd lost, but overboard he went. First, he brought up a beer can for my inspection. I stamped my foot and shook my head. "Nope, that's not it, Andre." So down he went again. This time he surfaced with a rusty old bucket. Again I stamped my foot. Undiscouraged, he retrieved a scallop shell and then a fishing rod, complete with reel. Finally he found that hammer, and my triumphant "That's it, Andre!" was received with obvious pleasure and relief.

And then one day in early fall, Luke Allen, working on his wharf, lost his favorite screwdriver overboard. When he mentioned the loss to me later that day, I called in Andre, who, at my signaled direction, went right to work. His first treasure was a fine imported wineglass; then in rapid order he came up with an interesting assortment of cultch that included a length of rope, a dog collar, and, of all things, a sackful of dead kittens, all of which I rejected. Finally, he appeared with what he thought must certainly be the prize. In his teeth, held precariously by its narrow rim, was a two-pound unopened can of grease. I didn't have the heart to tell him after this prodigious effort that his was a failed mission. A few days later, I was diving in that area and learned the reason for his failure: The screwdriver was buried deep in a bed of kelp.

It was in the fall of that year that I had a call from Charles Kuralt of CBS. He wanted to do a segment on Andre's fall release for his "On the Road" series. Busy as I was, I agreed to cooperate. Furthermore, I took time to help him line up a lobsterman for some footage on that Maine profession.

First, I approached Phil Raines, a rough-and-ready, freethinking Camden lobster-catcher. I'd dived for Phil on a number of occasions when he'd lost his mooring over the winter. I figured he'd be an ideal subject. (Straight-faced, Phil once had told some innocent summer people who wondered what he used for bait that most generally he used bricks soaked in kerosene, and if that didn't work, he tried peanuts.)

Phil listened impassively to Kuralt's pitch on his plan to capture on film something of the life of a hearty Maine lobsterman. "Guess I wunt," Phil said. Kuralt continued to press Phil, and when he saw he wasn't getting anywhere, he added a little sugar to his proposal: "Mr. Raines," he said, "we will pay you well for your time."

Phil didn't bat an eye. "Guess I wunt," he repeated. And I was forced to find a more flexible lobsterman to handle the assignment.

Later, it struck me that CBS hadn't offered to pay me for *my* time, nor had a half-dozen or more magazines that had asked me in recent years to cooperate with them. I decided then and there that Andre and I didn't need any more publicity, particularly exposure that entailed fattening someone else's pocketbook at the expense of mine. When a national magazine wrote and asked me to lend myself to its plans, I flatly turned it down.

The winter of 1973 was relatively easy, so I saw quite a bit of Andre. For the most part, he hauled out on Howard Kimball's float. Elray was away at school, but Howard, long resigned to accepting Andre's squatter's rights, was company. Not that Howard had the time to socialize, but at least he would talk to him and acknowledge his presence.

Most of the Rockport fishermen displayed admirable patience with the honorary harbormaster, but there was one notable exception. I have no way of knowing why Andre made Charlie his special mark. Perhaps, kid–like, he picked on the worst crank because he always was assured of a quick reaction. Whatever the reason, Andre plagued Charlie outrageously. Charlie had a cockleshell of a tender, and Andre never failed to nip at the oars when Charlie tried to row ashore from his lobster boat after a hard day tending traps. Like most fishermen, Charlie couldn't swim, a fact that made the trip to shore even more uncomfortable.

Charlie approached me one day, and he was wrathy. He told me that he'd a mind to shoot that blankety-blank seal. I said quietly that he'd better not do that. I didn't like the idea of giving in to that sort of threat, but I decided in the best interests of all concerned to put Andre back into his pen until things simmered down.

Then in the spring of 1973, a number of things happened to convince me something had to be done about Andre, for his own good, as well as in the interest of humankind, with whom he shared his sea pastures.

One fine May afternoon, two young men were canoeing in the outer harbor. Andre appeared to frolic, and in his playful exuberance, capsized the canoe. Fortunately, the young fellows were good swimmers. They swam ashore and passed off the incident as a lark. They might well have been youngsters who could not swim, in which event a tragedy might have resulted.

A few weeks later, a couple was kayaking home from Camden. The pair was still a mile from home with dark coming on when Andre joined them. With Andre nipping at their paddles and making terrier dashes at and under the frail craft, they could make no headway, and were in grave danger of being dumped into the sea. They finally did make it home to report the rather hairy adventure.

Then there was the matter of Andre's love affair with scuba divers. I suspect there was something more to this attachment than a delight in aquatic company; Andre had been suckled on neoprene, and indeed, there is something quite seal-like about a man swathed in that black, rubbery material. Most of the local divers knew Andre, were accustomed to his presence, and even enjoyed his company. But the sport was attracting hordes of new addicts, many of them tyros. On a number of occasions strangers to our waters were all but startled out of their wet suits when suddenly confronted with a bewhiskered face peering into their faceplates. I feared that one day a green diver might panic when thus accosted four fathoms down.

I was concerned about Andre as well. Many of these new divers carried spear guns and might well consider a seal bent on playing leapfrog fair game. At this time I didn't know quite what I was going to do, but it was clear that I no longer could be responsible for a seal who loved people not wisely, but too well.

I put Andre into his pen in late May, and during the summer months I weighed his future. In late August I arrived at a decision. What I had in mind was a gamble all the way, but it was a gamble I knew I had to take.

I phoned the New England Aquarium in Boston. I spoke to Lou Garibaldi, a member of the scientific staff whom I knew slightly. Not certain that Garibaldi remembered me, I introduced myself: "I'm Harry Goodridge in Rockport, Maine—the fellow with the seal, Andre."

If he didn't remember me, the mention of Andre made an immediate connection. I went right to the point, explaining my problem. "How would you like a winter boarder?" I asked him.

Without any hesitation Garibaldi said, "If you are talking about Andre, no problem. We'd be delighted. Just tell us when, and we'll come up with a truck and get him. And we'll return him to Rockport by truck in the spring."

I said, "Don't bother to deliver him in the spring. Just release him. Let him swim home."

There was a pause. "Did you say let him swim home, two hundred miles, in strange waters?"

"Andre's been around," I said. "If he wants to come home, he'll come home."

"How sure are you he'll want to come home?" Garibaldi asked.

"He'll either come home or go wild," I said. "We'll find that out in the spring, won't we?"

Andre waits in his crate for his trip to spend the winter at the New England Aquarium in Boston. (Lew Dietz)

Annie Potts became Andre's friend and trainer during his winter sojourn in Boston. (New England Aquarium)

Andre (left) with some friends from the New England Aquarium. (Goodridge Collection)

15

Boston Adventure

The light van from the New England Aquarium arrived around noon on that first day of November. Out stepped a pretty young woman who introduced herself as Annie Potts, the assistant trainer who would be looking out for Andre. With her was Bob Anderson, a member of the aquarium staff.

Andre sensed that something was afoot when the work boat nosed up to his pound with the carrying cage in the bow, but he flopped into the slatted box without any fuss, and remained composed as we brought it ashore and dragged it up the ramp to the van.

Annie, already displaying motherly concern about Andre's well-being, asked if there were any special instructions. If Andre didn't adjust to the aquarium situation, if he showed any signs of sickness or lassitude, she was not to try to treat him. "Just release him in the sea and notify me," I told her.

"You mean that?" Annie asked, a bit dismayed.

"I mean exactly that. He hasn't been protected like your aquarium seals. He knows his way around. But I think he'll be all right for a few·months if he has company."

"He'll be with three other harbor seals, a male and two females."

"That's fine," I said, "but, as a matter of fact, I was thinking of people company."

Annie smiled. "He'll have that, too. He'll have me, for one."

Reassured by her obvious fondness for animals, I pushed my head against Andre's cage to say good-bye. He nuzzled my hair, but that was all. He seemed relaxed, or perhaps "resigned" is the word; he had been through some pretty weird experiences with me over the years. What was it this time? he wondered.

When the van rolled off up the steep pitch to the village, I did feel a few pangs. After all those years of freedom, how would he adjust to the sterile confines of a tank? I told myself that he had adapted to all sorts of new situations over the years, and that he would adjust to this one. In any case, there was no point in worrying; I had had no alternative but to do what I had done. If things didn't work out, they would simply release him.

I suppose I was acting like a mother who has sent her kid off to summer camp for the first time. When several days had passed and I'd had no report of Andre's safe arrival, I phoned the aquarium and asked for the curator, Lou Garibaldi.

Lou was reassuring. "Everything is fine, Harry," he told me. "Everyone has fallen in love with Andre. Matter of fact, that seal of yours has taken over the place."

Lou went into some detail on the subject. One of the female seals had attached herself to Andre. Originally, she had been extremely shy, refusing to approach the handlers to be hand-fed. Quickly Andre had gentled her. Andre would slide right up on the stand to be fed, and soon his adoring admirer was doing likewise.

"But there is one small problem, Harry," Lou went on to say. "The male seal is named Hoover, and Hoover isn't at all happy about Andre taking over the two girls. He goes to the bottom of the pool and sulks. He hasn't been eating. I think we're going to have to put him in another tank."

Despite the good reports from Boston, I wasn't completely satisfied: I wanted to see for myself. I flew there in late January to pay Andre a visit. I confess I liked a reason to run down to Boston. I still have the wide-eyed, country-boy feeling of excitement walking the streets of a big city. Boston was the only city I knew as a kid growing up in nearby Salisbury. After I got my first driver's license, I remember heading into Boston. In those days driving a car in Boston was a hairy experience, and, always looking for a challenge, I wanted to prove that I could do it.

Going to Boston occasionally is still sort of a lark. I like to walk along Washington Street, pushing through the crowds and gawking. I like the feeling of having money in my pocket and going into the best restaurants for a few martinis and a money's-no-object sort of meal. I even enjoy sitting on the Boston Common and watching the silly pigeons.

That January day I went straight to the aquarium. The seal pool was outside at the entrance of the yet-to–be-completed grounds. I spotted Andre immediately. There he was, swimming about with his smaller lady friend in tow. I wandered over and said, "Hey there, Andre."

At the sound of my voice, Andre's head snapped around. He swam over to the edge of the pool and popped his head up for a closer look. Satisfied that I was the one and only Harry Goodridge, he went back to his consort. I noted that Andre was the lord of the manor; the lovelorn Hoover had been removed to other quarters.

That afternoon, at Annie Potts's suggestion, I put Andre through his paces. I did what I could with the few props that were available. Andre was delighted once again to have his show on the road.

There is this bit of business where I boot him and he grabs my pant leg and won't let go until I say the word *fish*. He was in the act of tugging at my pant leg when a pair of hippie types wandered over. "Hey," I said, "this seal has my leg and won't let go until I say the magic word. You know the magic word?"

"Nope," one of the fellows said, walking away, "but I hope the hell he pulls you overboard."

Annie Potts was, in fact, pulled overboard while I was coaching her in the business of getting Andre to leap through a hoop. Andre, doubtless seeing his chance for some fun, decided to hang up in the hoop. The sudden weight took Annie by surprise, and into the drink she went.

I was much relieved to find Andre in such good shape, both physically and emotionally. Annie told me later that he had become the darling of the staff. She was already feeling sad about the thought of his departure.

"He's so *human*," she said, adding quickly that perhaps she should not have said that as though it were a compliment. "I was feeding him one day, and the piece of fish was too small, I suppose. Anyway, he nipped my hand and drew a little blood. He was so solicitous and concerned. He kissed me and licked the wound. It was so touching, I almost cried."

After I'd been home a week or two, I had a phone call from my nephew, Teddy Goodridge. Teddy had made a special trip to Boston with his children to see Andre. He had been to Rockport many times, and the two had become close friends. In fact, Teddy had helped me in Andre's early training, and frequently made a point of coming to Rockport for the last show of the summer season to handle Andre so I could see the performance with the crowd. Teddy, a hulking bear of a fellow, has a shock of red hair and a wild sense of humor to go with it. On one occasion, Teddy, with the help of Ben

Allen, capped the season by tossing me into the pen with Andre. As I scrambled out of the chilly water, I overheard a lady in the audience ask, "Do they do that at every performance?" I put the lady straight: "No, ma'am," I told her, "only when they think the show needs a laugh."

Teddy reported on his trip to the aquarium. He'd introduced himself to Janey Shannon, who was working with Andre at the time. Andre had recognized him at once.

"I put Andre through a few of his tricks, then stood by while Janey worked with him. There were some sea lions in the tank, and one of them obviously was vying with Andre for status. I could see that he'd been top banana for some time, and he was determined to show the newcomer who was kingpin around the place.

"Janey would throw a collar into the pool and both Andre and this sea lion would go for it. Each time, the sea lion would beat Andre to it by a fraction of a second. He'd come up with it around his neck and lord it all over Andre. I could see that Andre was getting madder and madder. Finally, when Janey threw the collar and again the sea lion came up with it, Andre had taken about enough of it. He streaked to the bottom of the tank and muckled onto a large rubber mat. The thing must have weighed a good two hundred pounds. Andre dragged it up from the bottom and right up onto the stand. Then he looked down at the sea lion in the water as if to say, 'Let's see you match that, you two-bit SOB!'

"By that time quite a crowd had gathered. They all clapped and cheered. Andre was some self-satisfied, I can tell you. I doubt if that sea lion ever did get over it."

As the time approached for Andre's release, again I began to worry a little. I still had no doubt whatever that the Old Mariner was capable of making the two-hundred-mile journey, but after six months' confinement, would he opt to come home? It was all right with me if he exercised his free choice and decided to return to the wild. What disturbed me was that, in the event he didn't return to Rockport, I would never know if that was his choice, or if some ill had befallen him en route.

I had no fear of Andre's falling prey to natural enemies; he had none. There was hardly anything in the sea that would attack him, or if something did, he in his prime could avoid or handle it. For years, I'd read accounts of the dread killer whale's penchant for indiscriminate slaughter. According to these chilling tales, dozens of dolphins and seals had been found in a single killer's stomach. The myth of the killer whale's ferocity has been thoroughly exposed in recent years, largely because of man's efforts to get to know him. I've talked to aquarists who have gone into a tank with killer whales and found them playful. On the West Coast, a seal was put into a tank with a two-ton orca. The killer made a friend of the tender morsel.

My only fear for Andre lay in his inordinate love of man, and the chance of man's misunderstanding or exploiting that friendliness. In short, I had come to trust seals more than I trusted people.

The release was set for April 26. A few days before I was to leave for Boston, I got word out to the newspapers. Previously I hadn't said too much about my plan to release Andre in Boston, but now I wanted publicity: I wanted everyone along that stretch of New England coast to know that a friendly seal would be making his way north to Rockport.

I made a special point of alerting Jim Moore, then the district writer-photographer for the *Portland Press Herald*. Jim had been Andre's Boswell from the start, faithfully recording his adventures. The news stories precipitated a controversy over Andre's chances, and bets were made on the waterfront, the odds for the most part being against his returning home.

The forthcoming seal odyssey engaged scientific as well as

public interest. Jim Moore interviewed David Richardson, a friend of mine, and a biologist with the Maine Department of Marine Resources. Dave was too much of a scientist to make a prediction, but he did wish Andre well. "I hope he makes it," Dave said. "If it weren't for Harry, people in Maine might never have learned what a smart and friendly animal a harbor seal is."

So far as I could tell, I was the only one in Maine who would lay odds on Andre; but then, no one knew that seal as well as I did.

When I arrived at the aquarium that morning in April, I learned that the plans for the release had been revised. Lou Garibaldi was afraid that there might be some public outcry if Andre were released in polluted Boston Harbor, and in the midst of the marine traffic.

"If it's all right with you, we'll take him twenty miles north to Marblehead and let him go there."

I told him that was fine with me. In fact, I was delighted. Andre had been to Marblehead as a pup and, for all I knew, many times since. Homing from Marblehead would be a milk run for the Old Mariner. But the other thing the staff suggested *wasn't* fine with me. They hoped I would agree to have Andre harnessed with a radio transmitter so he could be tracked.

I shook my head. "Not a chance. In the first place, he doesn't need to be tracked; either he comes home or he goes wild. What does he need that electronic gear for? Why, that seal was born with more-sophisticated equipment than man will ever dream up. Secondly, Andre doesn't like a harness, and this is *his* adventure."

Since it had been agreed from the start that I would call the shots, Garibaldi agreed reluctantly that Andre would set forth unencumbered.

We drove to Marblehead in the van. Annie Potts was in Florida

at the time, so one of her coworkers was assigned as Andre's atten-
dant. During the trip she sat at his side, head bent, not speaking a
word. It might have been Andre's last rites for all her solemnity.

We were met at Marblehead by a battery of local and Boston
newsmen and photographers, as well as representatives from all the
wire services. For the first time that day, Andre began to act a bit
restive. He had been accustomed to attention, but nothing like this.
For that matter, I was a bit edgy myself.

The aquarium had arranged for the charter of a forty–foot
fishing boat. The skipper, a rugged young fellow, was waiting for us
at the dock. Waiting too were my nephew Teddy and my brother
Jake, who had come down from Salisbury for what they called the
"launchin'."

Andre was loaded aboard and followed by the aquarium personnel and the press. The big engine caught, the screw boiled the
black water, and we headed out against an easy swell.

We were in the outer harbor. I looked at Garibaldi. "Well,
what do you think?"

"What do you think?"

"What's wrong with right here?" I asked. I opened the door of
Andre's cage and he backed out. He explored the boat a few minutes,
then humped up on the washboards. He looked at me, then down at
the water, and *swoosh*, he was gone.

A half-minute later he surfaced. He looked around as though
getting his bearings. I called out across the water, "Okay, Andre, go
on home."

Andre dived again. He came up once more, then disappeared.
The crowd lined the rail, waiting for another glimpse of him. When
he didn't appear, I said, "That's it. We can all go home now." It was
1:30 p.m.

After an early supper, Jake and Teddy put me on the plane at Logan Airport. I chose a port seat on the little Piper Navaho that makes the run from Boston to Rockland. It was still light enough to see the fringe of coast as the plane flew over water. I could see the brown shoals, tucked-in harbors, toy boats scrawling white wakes on the dark silk of the sea, Gloucester, the crooked arm of Cape Ann, the Isles of Shoals, and Boon Island, where shipwrecked sailors in the seventeenth century had resorted to cannibalism. Dusk was settling in as we cleared the islands of Casco Bay. When the plane slid into the runway at Owls Head, it was dark.

In a brief hour, my overflight had covered the route Andre would take—was now taking. Would he make it a leisurely journey, swimming in the dark depths by night, resting and hunting by day? Would he savor his freedom, poking into coves and harbors, luxuriating in the feel of the tide, the sight and the rich smells of flats and seaweed; or would he set a course for home and hew to it with all deliberate speed? Whatever he decided, I wished him well.

I'd left my car at the airport. I drove it through the spring night, tired, yet curiously elated. It was as though I were involved in this odyssey, a party to this strange and stirring adventure.

Thalice and Toni were waiting when I walked into the house. They looked at me, questioning, not speaking.

"He's on his way," I said.

For this trip to Boston, Andre got an upgrade from car to plane. (Goodridge Collection)

Rockport lobstermen learned to tolerate Andre's appropriations of their boats and gear for napping. (Goodridge collection)

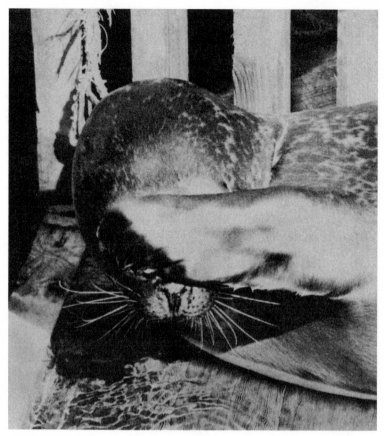

Andre was a natural ham. When performing, Harry's reprimand of "Shame on you!" would cause Andre to abashedly cover his face with his flipper—much to the delight of his audience. (Stan Waterman)

16

Seal Odyssey

The waiting began. Toni asked the question that had been asked by others, one that I had asked myself: How long would it take Andre to make it home? I had no way of knowing. I could say only that two weeks seemed like a reasonable span of time. What I meant, I expect, was that if two weeks passed and Andre didn't appear, I would be concerned.

The Maine skippers of the windships who took that sea route in the last century relied on the prevailing westerlies to carry their vessels downwind, or "down east," to Maine. They knew every rock and shoal, the set of the tides; night or day, the compass pointed at magnetic north to correct to a northeasterly course.

What senses and systems Andre would use to find his way home, I did not know. Little is known about animal navigational systems. How migrating birds find the way to their nesting grounds is still a mystery. Some suggest they get their clues from the sun, compensating in flight for the changing angle of the sun as the day progresses. You set a crab on high ground and it runs unerringly to the nearest water, no one is sure why or how. A hound will find his way home from some strange and distant spot where he has been taken by car. There are theories aplenty attempting to explain the mysterious internal systems by which creatures navigate and find home, but conclusive answers are not forthcoming.

Andre was capable of matching the speed of sailing ships under full canvas and the press of a fair wind. He could swim at fifteen knots in short sprints and cruise perhaps at ten. But surely Andre would not be "running" home. He would need to surface for oxygen; like a submarine, he would need to recharge his internal systems. He would need to hunt for food. And, certainly, he would, like any traveler, feel an urge to take sightseeing side trips on the way. Yet all the while he would know where he was and where he was heading: Some deep knowing would bring him home to Penobscot Bay where he was born.

The day after his release was a Saturday. I was home at my desk when the first call came. A man phoned from Kittery Point, roughly fifty miles north of Marblehead. He said his name was Norman Waddington.

"You the fellow with the seal, Andre?"

"Yes, I'm Harry Goodridge."

"I think I saw your seal. He was resting on my float. I went over and patted him."

"If you patted him, that was Andre all right," I assured him. "What time was this?"

"Two forty-five this afternoon. I went to get my camera, and when I got back he was swimming away out to sea. He has something on his back."

"'What sort of something?"

"Don't know, rightly. Just a glob of some kind. It wouldn't come off, so I left it."

I thanked him and hung up. I was happy to learn that the Old Mariner was on his way, but that "something" on his back troubled me. Had those aquarium people decided to hang a radio transmitter on him after all?

I waited around all day Sunday, but no further word came through. Spring is a busy time in my line of work, but I decided to stand watch at home and let my crew take care of my business. It was well that I did. I was finishing my breakfast Tuesday morning a little before 8:00 when the office phone rang. Gail Spear, who lived at Glen Cove, just down the line, had just spotted a seal off her shore where she had never before seen a seal. I thanked her but discounted the possibility that she had spotted Andre.

Wondering, I took my coffee to my desk and consulted the navigation chart of the New England coast. Andre had been sighted Saturday morning at Kittery Point, fifty miles north of Marblehead. The fact that I had had no reports for three days could mean that he might have gone offshore and taken the direct route for a landfall somewhere near Monhegan Island, and then come straight up Penobscot Bay. If indeed that had been Andre at Glen Cove, he hadn't dawdled: He'd come fast on a homing course. But in less than four days? I still couldn't believe it.

I was wrong in my skepticism. At 9:00 a.m., not much more than an hour after the call from Glen Cove, the phone rang again. Louis Bosse of Owls Head, the arm of land just south of Rockport, had sighted the Old Mariner. He said he was certain it was Andre who had been resting on the rocks at Cooper's Beach. Now I *was* certain. And when a lobsterman phoned an hour later to tell me that seal of mine was swimming around in Rockland Harbor, all doubts vanished.

I phoned Jim Moore to alert him to the imminent arrival of Rockport's illustrious citizen, and then took some fish out of the freezer to thaw. I hurried down to the waterfront to check the harbor.

I was back at the house for lunch when the kitchen phone rang. Thalice answered it. On the line was Una Ames, who lives across the harbor with her husband, Leonard, next door to Howard Kimball. It was 1:30 p.m., four days almost to the minute from the time Andre had been released at Marblehead.

"He's here," Una fairly shouted. "He's resting in Leonard's skiff. I called to him and I think he waved a flipper at me."

I grabbed the bucket of fish and raced down to my boat. Sure enough, there was Andre in full possession of Leonard Ames's skiff. He bestirred himself at the sound of the approaching outboard, raising his head over the gunwale of the half-swamped little boat.

"Hello there, Andre," I said in a conversational voice. "How was the trip?"

He gazed at me owlishly a moment; then, with the magnificent insouciance of a grand monarch, he went back to his nap. Nor did he show any interest in the fish I had brought to celebrate his safe arrival. He might as well have said in the manner of an arriving summer guest, "Thanks just the same, but I had lunch on the plane."

So I patted him briefly and left him to rest up from his journey.

An hour or so later, Luke Allen called the house to say that Andre was in the inner harbor and seemed to want to get into his pound. There he was waiting when I arrived on the scene. I pushed out in my boat and opened the gate of his pound. Without any hesitation, he humped up on the deck and slid into his private pool. Andre was home.

It was then that I saw the strange glob on his back. I called him over and examined it carefully. I was stumped. I went home and returned with a pair of shears and cut it loose from his fur. Later I looked at the mass under a glass and even went so far as to slice off a section of it. Finally, I immersed it in a bottle of alcohol with the idea of mailing it to a scientist friend for identification.

Instead, I decided to phone the aquarium. It was unlikely that the aquarium staff would have encumbered Andre with some secret electronic device after our discussion, but I wanted to be sure.

A woman answered the phone. "Oh, that," she said, laughing, after I'd described the mysterious substance. "That's bubblegum. Just as Andre was leaving the aquarium some kid stepped up and slapped his wad of gum on Andre's back. 'That's so the guy in Maine will know this is the right seal when Andre gets home,' he announced."

"Smart kid," I muttered, but it was only later, when the full irony of it struck me, that I smiled. Bubblegum! The civilization Andre had adopted had finally caught up with him. Andre was quite unaware of the indignity to which he had been subjected. I'm sure it wouldn't have bothered him unduly if he'd known about it. Andre knew who and what he was; he could afford to be serene. Seals had been seals long before man's ancestors had had the wit to climb down out of trees.

I remember something the naturalist Loren Eiseley wrote in his delightful book, *The Immense Journey*. He said whimsically that he had long been an admirer of the octopus. "They are," he wrote, "the wisest of mollusks. . . . I have always felt it to be just as well for us that they never came ashore."

We need have no fear of the seal's forsaking the good sea life for a harsh terrestrial existence. After Andre's return I wondered what he had learned of value in his fourteen years of association with man. Not much, I concluded. On the other hand, what I had learned about sealdom from my friend Andre was of value beyond price.

I wandered down to see Andre after supper that evening. A warm southerly blew in from the sea. Villagers were busy scraping and painting their boats, preparing for another spring. Andre still refused my proffered handout of frozen fish, so I lighted my pipe and, like the walrus and the carpenter, we sat there in the dusk and talked of many things.

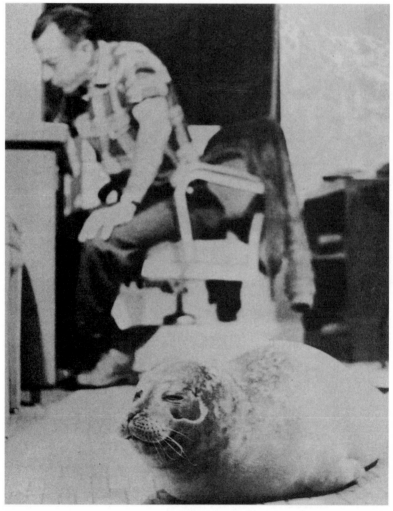

Harry working, Andre dozing. Andre never did understand that, unlike harbor seals, people have to work for a living. (Stan Waterman)

17

The Feds Come to Call

February 11, 1975. I sit at my desk, working on bills and looking out at a Christmas-card village. Snow fell in the night, a wet snow, whiter than white, that mantles the roofs and clings in cottony tufts to the bare trees.

Groundhog Day, February 2, has come and gone. That is the day the chubby marmot, known in Maine as the woodchuck, emerges from its den to check on the signs of spring. This year there was no sun to cast a shadow on that day. If there is truth in the ancient myth, spring is around the corner. Maine people are not beguiled by that fable: They have come to learn that spring comes when the peepers sing in the bogs, and not before.

I think about my friend Andre. He left for his winter sojourn in late October. He will swim home to Rockport in the spring. What adventures or misadventures will befall him en route are yet to be logged. I am anxious to see him and more than ready for another spring.

Unlike a fiction, a true relation cannot be arranged with a proper beginning, middle, and end. One can say only that this is the way it was. The end of Andre's story is not in sight. Looking back to the past summer, it did seem that our major problems had been solved. Andre would remain in his floating pen in the summer and go to Boston in the fall, to return with the birds in the spring.

I don't suppose Andre thinks there is anything special about a seal who goes to Boston for the winter and swims home in the spring. He accepts things as they are. I saw no sign that he fretted in his confinement last summer. He had visitors aplenty, of course. Each day dozens of boats nosed up to his quarters to say hello. Andre is a celebrity. But fame has its penalties, as I was to learn before the summer was over.

I was getting out of my car one day in late July when three men approached me. One of them flashed his identification folder. He was, he informed me, chief enforcement officer for the National Marine Fisheries Service. He was based at Gloucester; the other two men were enforcement officers from Portland and Rockland, respectively.

For the life of me I couldn't imagine what I'd done to warrant the attention of not one but three federal agents. I asked them what I could for for them.

"We'd like to see your seal," the Gloucester man said. "You might very well be in violation of the federal law. Are you aware of the Marine Mammal Protection Act of 1972?"

I told him that of course I was aware of that law; moreover, I thought it a good law. "But, look here," I said, "I had Andre years before that law was on the books. In the spring and fall, Andre comes and goes as he pleases. He just got back from Boston a few months ago."

"We know all that," the head man said. "We've known about this situation for some time. But we're not at all sure you're relieved by any grandfather clause. You let the seal out of the pen. Right?"

"Right."

"Then he comes back and goes into the pen?"

"Right."

"So, legally that would constitute a recapture. You still may well be in violation."

That bit of slick legal folderol made me blink; I was confused, and then angry. "Why," I asked, "if you knew all about this situation, has it taken you so long to pounce?"

I saw that the question was embarrassing.

"We've had complaints," the fellow muttered. "A woman in the region wants to keep a seal. She wonders, if you can keep a seal, why she cannot. Now, if you don't mind, we'd like to see your seal."

I did mind, but in the face of such a show of authority, I didn't think I had any alternative but to comply with that official request. The feds couldn't have picked a more inopportune time to inspect Andre. He was half through his shedding time; his normally glossy coat was dull and mottled. But I took the delegation out to the pen and simply said, "Well, here he is."

They looked things over for a few minutes and, to my surprise, made no comment on his less than prime appearance. Sharp legal beagles they may be, I thought, but they don't know anything about seals.

As they were about to depart, I said, "I don't know if you have a leg to stand on, but in any event, I think you should know that if this gets into the papers, your bureau is in for some embarrassment."

The agent didn't take this gentle threat too well. "I think we can handle that all right," he told me.

And of course the press did get wind of the story. I had no doubt that the media would find a confrontation between an inno-cent seal and the big bad feds irresistible, but I was totally unprepared for the volume and intensity of the public clamor that ensued.

It began with a lead piece in the *Portland Press Herald*. The cry was taken up by the local and regional press. On August 2, under a *Portland Press Herald* front-page banner headline—ANDRE SEAL IN BIG TROUBLE WITH FEDS—district correspondent David Himmelstein wrote, "Rockport's honorary harbormaster may be forcibly removed from office—and his home—because a federal law prohibits the capture of marine mammals."

The next day, under the headline ANDRE GAINS CIVIC GROUP BACKING, the same newspaper printed the reactions of a number of the region's civic leaders: "We're going to do everything we can to maintain Andre's status quo in Rockport," said Sandy Graffam, chairman of the board of selectmen. "If necessary, we'll file a letter of appeal with federal officials."

"We don't even consider him a wild animal—he's more of a town character," asserted Helen Parker, executive secretary of the Camden-Rockport Chamber of Commerce.

Letters poured in to me and, presumably, to the National Marine Fisheries Service office. The feds were called pigheaded blunderers, busybodies and bureaucrats, and worse. Editorial pages took up the *cause célèbre*, and two local lawyers offered to take Andre's case free of charge.

By the end of August, the Save Andre passion had reached fever pitch. Into the fray stepped Maine's congressman Peter Kyros, senior senator Ed Muskie, and junior senator Bill Hathaway. In a letter directed to the Secretary of Commerce, under whose wing the National Marine Fisheries Service nests, Senator Hathaway wrote, "Andre appears quite content with his summer residence in Rockport, and I believe in this instance the good of the public as well as the seal would be served if Andre is permitted to decide for himself where he will live."

Though doubtless staggered by this unexpected public reaction, the feds held their ground. They phoned me one day to say that I should apply for a permit, and that the matter of its disposition would be taken under advisement. A few days later, I received another phone call, during which I was told to hold off applying for a permit. Completely confused by then, I decided to hold *my* ground. Finally, on the last day of September, the feds surrendered.

On that day a letter arrived. The director of the National Marine Fisheries Service began by restating the federal law and ended by informing me of the Service's decision: "Subsequent to our investigation of this matter, we submitted the question to our Office of General Counsel. We have recently been advised by our attorneys that, on the basis of an old and unique body of law relating to the animal's intention to return to its master, Andre was owned prior to December 21, 1972. Therefore, you do not need a permit to hold and display Andre."

Later I learned that this "old and unique body of law" went back to Colonial days. Though a farmer's cow may go wild, the original owner holds proprietary rights to her, since there is presumptive evidence that the cow intends to return. However, by accepting such rights, the farmer must also accept the responsibility for any damage the vagrant cow might commit while on the loose.

I am wondering how I can explain these fine legal points to Andre. We both know that I neither hold nor wish to hold proprietary rights to him. In a matter of months I will journey to Boston to see him off for Maine. He will slip into the water, and I will say, "Go home, Andre." I will then go home and wait to see if it is his intention to return.

Maine Governor Brennan makes peace with Andre. Perhaps it was Andre's endorsement that gave the governor such a comfortable margin in his reelection bid. (Courtesy Rockland Historical Society, Jim Moore Collection)

Among his accolades,
Andre was named
Townsperson of the Year
(above) and Honorary
Rockport Harbor Master
(right). (Jim Moore)

Old friends. (Rockland Courier Gazette)

Epilogue, 1975

May 1. Andre was released yesterday before noon in Marblehead Harbor. I sit in my office by the phone with my breakfast coffee. Andre's floating pen is overboard and ready. I have stocked some herring in my freezer. The newspapers have been alerted. The *Portland Press Herald* has asked its readers along the coast to participate in the Spot-Andre Watch and report sightings. There is little I can do now but wait.

The release went smoothly and according to plan. A small crowd was gathered when we arrived at Marblehead in the aquarium truck. We lugged Andre to the town float in his carrying cage, and I simply opened the door and said, "Okay, the ocean is all yours, Andre. Go along home." He took to the water like a kid to the old swimming hole. He didn't head out to sea at once as he had last spring. He was still cavorting around the harbor when I left at about 1:00 p.m.

The first bulletin comes in. I have word that Andre remained in Marblehead Harbor for five hours. He was last seen racing a woman in a small sailboat. Then, in the early evening, he was spotted in Manchester Harbor, a few miles north of Marblehead. Bill Loring, a local yachtsman, waved to him, and Andre, taking this as an invitation, tried to climb aboard his boat, but was promptly discouraged.

May 2. The first Maine report came in this afternoon from James Lash of Boothbay Harbor. Lash told the *Press Herald* he had sighted a friendly seal in Linekin Bay. "He was diving, rolling, and generally cavorting," Lash reported. When the paper phoned me, I said that it couldn't be Andre. More than a hundred miles in twenty-four hours!

May 3. I was wrong about that. I had a call at seven this morning from Keith Monaghan of Port Clyde, which is just west of Rockport. Monaghan and another fisherman, Henry Benner, had spotted Andre asleep in Benner's punt. "But you better hurry down here with a pair of heavy wire cutters. That seal of yours has been carrying a pound diamond jig. I cut the jig free, but the treble hook is still snagged in his upper lip."

I rushed over to Port Clyde. Andre recognized my voice and came to me like a streak. He suffered patiently while I cut out two of the prongs. The other was too deeply embedded, and I knew I'd need a vet. So I slapped his back and said, "Go along home now, Andre. I'll be waiting."

May 4. Andre arrived home at dawn today. He made the almost 200-mile trip in somewhat less than three days! I was roused out of sleep before seven, and there was Donny Grey, a local lobsterman, at my door. "Your seal is back," Donny told me. "He seemed to want to get into his pen. So I let him in."

I dressed and rushed down to the harbor with a ration of herring. Andre seemed delighted to see me and pleased to be home. But all he wanted to do was sleep. I phoned the New England Aquarium. They will send up a vet to operate and remove that metal prong. Then, when the Old Mariner is rested up, we'll talk things over and make some plans for the summer.

And now, as I sit looking out upon a warm spring evening and hearing the peepers singing in the bog, I decide to celebrate my friend's homecoming with a glass of good scotch whiskey.

Many a Rockport summer brought throngs of people who couldn't get enough of Andre's antics. (Goodridge Collection)

Andre was an honored guest—and the ringbearer—at Toni's wedding (above, courtesy Rockland Historical Society, Jim Moore Collection). And when Toni's daughter married, Andre was there in spirit (left). (Goodridge Collection)

Afterword, 2014

It was more than fifty years ago when our father first set the new-born Andre down on our back lawn. Accustomed to taming wild creatures, seals among them, we were not overly impressed by the latest family member. But like a kitten or puppy, a baby seal has charms that are hard to resist, and we were not immune. We joined in the nurturing, weaning, and raising of this adorable creature. We swam with him, visited him in his various enclosures as he grew, and, throughout his life, followed Dad's reports of his training, exploits, media coverage, bad behavior, disappearances, and homecomings.

While we were aware of Andre's growing fame over the years, we took him for granted as we might have a spoiled younger brother. We didn't fully realize how remarkable the relationship between Andre and Harry was until both of them were gone. Looking back now on the entire course of their friendship, we marvel at the enduring bond of trust they shared and the unique life Dad both caused and allowed Andre to live.

After the 1975 publication of *A Seal Called Andre*, this bond remained unbroken for eleven more years. During the summer months, Dad and Andre continued their performances at feeding time for each evening's assembled spectators. The homegrown quality of the performance—an old tire in place of a hoop to jump through, Dad pulling his own handkerchief from his pocket when he told Andre to blow his nose—set it apart from more sophisticated animal acts and endeared it to audiences for twenty-five years. Locals who were children at the time fondly recall watching the show with their families, or even "passing the bucket"—going through the crowd with a plastic pail to solicit donations to buy fish for Andre to eat. After each show was over, these kids went back to Dad's office to count the proceeds. They would then go home with their ten per-cent cut jingling in their pockets.

Dad's portion of the take always went into the fish budget, but in 1976 the need for a new pen prompted the diversion of these funds, resulting in the construction of a bigger and better floating home for Andre. Some larger donations from friends and fans helped in the effort, and there was even enough left over to upgrade Andre's mode of travel to Boston from truck to plane.

When it came time to make the annual trip that November, Andre was lifted in his crate aboard a small chartered plane. He showed no signs of anxiety, as if flying were as natural an activity for a seal as basking on a seaweed-covered ledge. Dad flew with him to Boston, where members of the aquarium staff picked up Andre and returned him to his winter residence in the city.

There he resumed his alpha-male role among the full-time seals, remaining until late April, when he was once again taken to Marblehead. Released on the shore, Andre flopped across the sand through a channel of cheering children. He entered the water, dipped under, surfaced, and scanned the horizon to assess the situa-tion. Dad stayed long enough to catch his eye and shout the token reminder, "Go home, Andre," before returning to Rockport to wait while the seal made his long northward journey.

In what had become a rite of spring, the Andre Watch had official-ly begun. People all along the coast kept their eyes peeled for a glimpse of a seal resting on a dock or a boat, and those lucky enough to spy one reported their sightings to Dad and the press. In 1977, Andre made the roughly one hundred eighty mile trip in four days. This was slower than his record speed of sixty-five hours, but a good deal faster than the year when, in no hurry or with some seal business to attend to, he took two weeks and traveled well beyond Rockport before turning back for home.

For years, Andre swam free nearly every day during the summer mating season. That privilege ended abruptly, however, when an ornery Andre attacked a man rowing with his wife in their twelve-foot boat. "Muckle," was the word the man used to describe how Andre grabbed his chest and arm after clambering over the gunwale and nearly swamping the boat. In spite of his lifelong contact with humans, Andre was still a wild animal who did not always behave politely or predictably.

While his days and seasons had a kind of rhythm, there was much in Andre's life that was not routine. As the subjects of numerous newspaper and magazine articles, radio interviews, and TV broadcasts—local, national, and even international—he and Dad gave many hours to reporters and photographers. And Dad constantly sought ways to showcase Andre's intelligence, working with him on new ideas to keep the seal from getting bored.

In the summer of 1977, The New England Aquarium sent Smoke, a lively and lovely female harbor seal, to join Andre in his new pen, with the hope that they might produce a baby Andre (or Andrea). The stay was intended to be brief, but was extended to October as the two seals developed an obvious fondness for one another. Dad taught Smoke a few tricks, which enhanced the daily show, but the romance failed to produce more than mutual adoration. After Smoke was returned to Boston, a lonely Andre paced back and forth underwater for days. The two were reunited at the aquarium that winter, and Smoke came back to Rockport in the spring for a few more months, but their love affair remained pup-less.

Late in the summer of 1978, Andre began training for the unveiling of his own statue. Jane Wasey, a well-known sculptor who lived locally, wished to immortalize Andre in stone, and her request to Rockport's town fathers to place a statue in the Marine Park was gratefully granted.

Starting with a four-ton slab of granite donated by a quarry in nearby Union, Ms. Wasey labored for over a year on her creation. She presented her gift to the people of the Town of Rockport in a public ceremony on a sparkling Sunday in October. While the high school band played and hundreds of people looked on, Harry released Andre from his pen as a volunteer on shore threw the rope attached to the sculpture's canvas covering into the water. "Get the rope, Andre," Dad commanded. Andre dove, came up with the rope's knotted end firmly in his teeth, and, swimming back toward his pen, pulled the cover off the statue to reveal a work of art that will endure for generations. Based on land yet looking forever seaward, the granite Andre embodies the seal's double life. The statue remains the focal point of the park, where visiting children are free to climb on its larger-than-life back and put their arms around its fat neck. But on that day, as the crowd cheered their approval, Andre was only interested in gulping down the juicy chunks of mackerel that were his reward for a job well done.

Speaking at a banquet for the Maine Press Association not long after the unveiling, Governor Joe Brennan stated that the media gave too much attention to the antics of Andre and not enough to what he considered the important issues of the day. One reporter heard gasps and noted dropping jaws. The next day's headlines—

"He Said What About Andre?", "Governor's Andre Speech Seals Fate")—caused such a pro-Andre uproar that, when he was running for re-election, Governor Brennan made the trip to Rockport from the State Capitol in Augusta to make amends with the wronged seal.

Standing with his honored guest on the platform inside the floating pen, Dad asked, "What do you think of the governor, Andre?" To the delight of onlookers, Andre snorted his famous raspberry. "Shame on you, Andre," Dad scolded, and Andre covered his eyes with a flipper. This brought forth an apology from the governor, who then leaned down to shake Andre's flipper. "Now show the governor what you really think of him," said Dad. Andre rapidly smacked his flippers on his wet belly, the governor fed him a chunk of herring, and all was forgiven. Brennan thanked Dad, who was a crusty independent in more than just politics and later remarked that Brennan and gotten some good mileage out of all the coverage. The governor went on to win the election by a comfortable margin.

In appreciation of the attention and tourists that Andre and Harry continued to bring to the area, the local Chamber of Commerce chose them as "Townspersons of the Year." The award ceremony took place at the stately Whitehall Inn in Camden— where Pulitzer Prize winning poet Edna Saint Vincent Millay gave her first public reading in 1912. On his big night, Andre entered the dining room, flopping to the podium behind Dad — and his bucket of fish, which had become a nearly permanent appendage. After reading a congratulatory telegram from Governor Brennan, the master of ceremonies presented a plaque to Dad and placed an engraved medallion on a leather collar around Andre's neck. Andre and Harry reciprocated with as much of their repertoire as they could perform without the benefit of water, and Andre, ever the crowd pleaser, left the podium several times to mingle with the audience. It would be difficult to invent a greater contrast in performances at the Whitehall than a lovely young woman delivering the eloquent lines of her poetry and a fat bull seal devouring raw fish.

Trainers at the New England Aquarium, with Dad's agreement, wanted to try an experiment to see if Cabot Spot, one of numerous abandoned seal pups raised at the aquarium, would follow Andre on his next trip from Massachusetts to Rockport. In order to familiarize him with Andre's world, the two seals would spend some time in Andre's Rockport pen and Cabot Spot would be released each day to learn the ways of the deep.

When Cabot Spot was introduced into the pen, Andre attacked him and pinned him underwater for several minutes. Once Andre had established his dominance and finally came up for air, Dad gave him a severe reprimand. From then on, the two seals coexisted without incident.

At first Cabot Spot had little interest in freedom, and when he was released outside the pen he would immediately return. Gradually, however, he got more comfortable with his aquatic surroundings, until one day he swam off and did not return. This loss of an animal "owned" by the aquarium led to a misunderstanding, so Dad decided to give Andre his freedom for the winter instead of returning him to Boston.

In the fall of 1980, Andre was chosen to be the ring bearer in a family wedding and dutifully rehearsed his role with Harry and our brother Steve. On a rainy October afternoon, Toni—the youngest of our parents' five kids—was married to Richard Lermond near the statue of Andre at Rockport Marine Park. With two hundred guests looking on, the father of the bride stood beside the couple in suit and tie with, of course, a bucket of fish. When it was time for the vows, Dad called Andre from the water and instructed him to "go get the rings." Andre vanished beneath the surface, swam to Steve, stationed underwater in Scuba gear, and returned a few moments later with a small pouch in his mouth. He presented the pouch to the best man, who produced the rings from within. Andre waited for the vows and the kiss, applauded with his flippers, then relinquished the spotlight and returned to the water.

Thirty-one years passed before Toni and Richard's daughter celebrated her own wedding in the same park, with the statue of Andre sporting a big white bow and a sign that read, "Congratulations Lara and Peter from Harry and Uncle Andre."

Andre spent the winter of 1981 again swimming free in Maine, but his habit of taking over rowboats, biting oars, and other potentially dangerous behavior once again compelled Dad to confine him for the winter months. In the fall, Andre was flown to Connecticut, where he settled in comfortably at the Mystic Aquarium and spent an uneventful few months.

In the spring, Dad felt no qualms about setting him free on the southern New England shore for a much longer trip home than he had ever made. He was confident that Andre could navigate the strange territory and that he would once again demonstrate the savvy intelligence that had served him well for twenty years.

When word got out that Andre would be swimming from Connecticut instead of Massachusetts, that he would have to negotiate the waters of the southern New England coast, go outside Cape Cod and cross a much longer stretch of open sea, critics accused Dad of being irresponsible and requested that he have Andre swim from familiar Marblehead. For once, Dad appeared to be swayed by public opinion, though in fact it was the influence of a few close advisers—his family included—that changed his mind.

He decided on a compromise, in which Andre would be flown to Provincetown, at the tip of Cape Cod, to start his swim. Whatever route he chose to take, he would not have to navigate the unknown territory and maritime dangers of Connecticut, Rhode Island, and southern Massachusetts. This quieted most of those opposed to any change in their beloved seal's itinerary.

Once again Dad's faith in Andre was rewarded. Five days after leaving Provincetown, he arrived at the security of his Rockport pen and entered it to rest.

Andre wintered in Mystic for three more years, swimming back to Rockport from Provincetown. Every trip elicited calls of reported sightings along his route, and each spring he returned home safely.

By 1985, the venerable animal was showing signs of his age and going blind from the cataracts that clouded his eyes. While he appeared able to function perfectly well underwater, his evening performances had to be modified to adapt to his declining eyesight. He could no longer see to jump through his hoop or interpret Dad's hand signals from the back of the pen.

That fall Andre returned to Mystic for the last time. It was obvious from his refusal to eat that he was unhappy, so, when the hunger strike was in its eleventh day, Dad made the six-hour drive to Mystic, loaded Andre in his car, and drove him home to Rockport, where he was released into the frigid, but familiar, December ocean.

With appetite restored, Andre spent his last winter and spring swimming free but staying close to home, until a day in early June when a bystander saw him attacked by a wild seal. Disadvantaged by age and blindness, Andre was defeated and driven out of his own Rockport Harbor, never to return.

Word spread quickly. Sightings of seals, alive and dead, were reported to Dad over a period of several weeks. He viewed a number of corpses, none of them Andre. Then one day in July he was called to Lermond Cove in nearby Rockland. There, washed up on the rocky shore, lay the body of Andre.

Dad, Steve, and Toni's husband Richard retrieved the body and buried it in the family animal cemetery. We chose a sleek gray headstone from the Rockport shore whose color and shape are reminiscent of a harbor seal. It bears the simple inscription:

ANDRE
1961 – 86

Andre was a captured wild animal who had the choice of remaining wild or living in captivity. For twenty-five years he chose both. The simple explanation for this could be that Andre had "imprinted" on Harry or was just taking advantage of free room and board. The deeper explanation involves qualities of intelligence and sensitivity in both seal and man that have not yet been measured and may never be.

Dad was a World War II veteran who, like many of that generation, kept most of his personal emotions private. A lifelong naturalist, he knew well that as every creature is born, so it must die. Even though he had hoped to outlive his seal companion, he couldn't completely conceal the feeling of loss he suffered when the focus of so much of his life for so long was no longer with him. He died four years later in early spring while planting peas in his garden.

The water was calm and the sky cloudless on the afternoon in July when Steve and Richard, in their lobster boats, transported sixteen family members out to Robinson's Rock, Andre's birthplace. In the silence that followed the cutting of the engines, we were surrounded by dozens of curious seals, who watched as we scattered Harry's ashes, along with lilies and forget-me-nots, over the glistening water. The seal and his man had come full circle — the ending back at the beginning.

— Harry's daughters:

> Susan Goodridge Crane
> Carol Goodridge
> Paula Goodridge Armentrout
> Toni Goodridge

The last photo taken of Andre before his death. (Goodridge Collection)